THE CO

"You might wonder why, as a parable writer who seldom concentrates on more than two or three 'secrets' at once, I would endorse *The Complete Leader*—a book that essentially teaches you everything you need to become a high performing leader. This book can serve as your own leadership curriculum as you work on the competencies you need to be an effective leader. You'll take the self assessment in the back of the book, decide which of the twenty-five leadership competencies you need help on, and then go to the appropriate chapter. Thanks, Ron and Randy, for putting all this valuable information in one place."
Ken Blanchard, coauthor of *The One Minute Manager®* **and** *Leading at a Higher Level*

"*The Complete Leader* encapsulates the lifelong learning of master practitioners and thought leaders on the subject. This masterpiece is an essential and insightful learning tool to fast forward the career for every aspiring great leader."
Imelda Butler, Odyssey Transformational Strategies, Dublin, Ireland

"No two people understand leadership better than Ron Price and Randy Lisk. They have been leading, teaching and coaching others to lead for years. Now, they have given us the complete guide. What a gift! Full of practical insights and terrific coaching, *The Complete Leader* will alter the performance of leaders worldwide."
John Hersey, President TTI Success Insights North America,
Author of *Creating Contagious Leadership*

"Having coached dozens of leaders, I believe that Ron and Randy have captured one critical component of every great leader: self-awareness. The most outstanding leaders understand themselves and each of the competencies that the authors explain so powerfully. This should be the one book that sits on every leader's – or soon to be leader's – desk."
Terri Kabachnick, CSP, CPBA, CPVA, CPHDA, CEO and
Founder, The Kabachnick Group, Inc.

"Whether you are a clerk or the manager of a store, the CEO of a corporation or even the president of a country, you will benefit from reading and applying the principles of *The Complete Leader.*"
Jim Zamzow, Zamzows Superstores

"This book comes at a time when society has recognized the need to go beyond knowledge acquisition and develop the whole person. By combining a thorough review of the literature, state of the art assessment tools, decades of personal experience by the authors and engaging life stories, *The Complete Leader* provides a common vocabulary that makes each required competency come alive. This is a must read for anyone on the path to complete personal development and should be required reading for every higher education student and professor."
Ron Bonnstetter, Ph.D., Professor Emeritus, University of Nebraska

"My Jewish tradition has a teaching: *"The main thing is not the expounding—it is the doing."* Ron Price and Randy Lisk embody that wisdom in their terrific new book, *The Complete Leader*. *The Complete Leader* is an extraordinary resource for all who seek to continually grow our leadership skills."

Rabbi Dan Fink, Ahavath Beth Israel, Boise, Idaho

"Many of us, when we think about the leaders that have influenced our careers, find it difficult to describe those traits or skills that make them so special and inspiring. Ron and Randy describe a set of 25 essential skills that separate exceptional leaders from the rest."

Jorge A. Perez-Martinez, D.V.M. Ph.D,
V.P. & General Manager, NE Asia Zoetis Japan

"One unique insight that Ron and Randy's book offers is many of the leadership traits discussed *overlap* between the business and personal world. The book offers more than another look at business; it is a guide to living a life as a leader."

Stuart Boylan, VP Business Development, Pacific Steel & Recycling

"*The Complete Leader* offers a complete nutrition to your lifelong leadership development with its unique approach of combining book, assessment and website."

Keith Choy, Regional General Manager, China/HK & Taiwan,
Pfizer Consumer Healthcare

"*The Complete Leader* is one of the best books on leadership that I have read."

David Butler, CEO North Canyon Medical Center

"Great book and really useful, cuts right to the chase! It's an extremely user-friendly guide in supporting one's never-ending quest in becoming the complete leader. This is the only how-to leadership book aspiring 'complete' leaders need on their desks."

Albert Wada, Chairman, Wada Farms

"In *The Complete Leader*, Ron and Randy have provided invaluable insight to all those who either aspire to leadership or strive to become more effective leaders. Leadership is not easy; I highly recommend *The Complete Leader* to anyone beginning their leadership journey or seeking to take their leadership skills to a new and exciting level."

Steven Berenter, Managing Partner, Hawley Troxell Ennis & Hawley LLP

"In 25 years leading teams with different cultures, I have never encountered a book about leadership that puts the concept in such a realistic and pragmatic way. It is highly beneficial that these concepts come from leaders like Ron and Randy, who have led organizations and have been able to connect the concepts with real-world experiences."

Jose Francisco (Paco) Ortiz Collado, Senior Vice President &
General Manager, Zoetis Brazil

"Leadership is an exhilarating, gut wrenching, often breathtaking journey that demands changing skills and lifelong learning. Ron and Randy have just provided a roadmap that should be a well worn reference on every leader's bookshelf."

Jeff Sayer, Director, Idaho Dept of Commerce

"*The Complete Leader* is actually written by leaders. I think this is extremely important to note in an era where everyone claims to be an expert. I personally consulted with Ron Price for guidance and leadership as I launched a new creative chapter to my life and work. His leadership paid off big time for me. I highly recommend you read this comprehensive road map on the implementation of stronger leadership."

Danielle Kennedy, Actress, Freelance Writer, Speaker

"*The Complete Leader* is a powerful and resourceful book that will benefit anyone who picks it up. As one of the developers of the TriMetrix® HD, I really appreciate how Ron and Randy take the 25 competencies and create a practical and sensible connection to leadership."

Rick Bowers, President, TTI Success Insights, International Division

"Like most leaders, I have a bedside stack of books that have been read once and set aside. I'm excited to now have a tailored learning system that digs deeper and promises to adapt to the ever-evolving work environment."

Callie Zamzow Novak, CEO, Dynamite Marketing, Inc.

"Ron Price's work has always been focused on practical application of knowledge in people's lives, and this book promises to do the same. As stated in the introduction, leadership is a journey, and the final test of a leader is their ability to transcend self-interest and self-promotion to serve a greater cause. A leader needs to be a lifelong learner, always seeking to better understand themselves and the people they serve."

Tom Dale, Mayor, City of Nampa (2001 – 2013)

"A must read, *The Complete Leader* provides as insightful and systemic approach toward enriching the competencies of leaders in their journey of development and growth."

Mark Kadell, President & CEO, Thomas Cuisine Management

"As Ron and Randy point out in the intro of the book, leaders are naturally incomplete and the joy of becoming a better leader is the constant journey of improvement. However, this is the most complete book on leadership I've ever read. As you read the book, you will often find yourself saying, 'I wish I had this book 10 years ago.'"

Justin Foster, Foster Thinking

"As a 'Gen Y' leader, I found this book to be unlike any other of its kind. No tired clichés or recycled materials—but practical and realistic insight constructed from years of experience that I am able to convert into practical use as a leadership beginner."

Sarah Turner, Director, TTI Success Insights U.K.

"Ron and Randy have many years of successful business leadership and consulting under their belts. If you are looking for deeper insight into the skills of a complete leader and how to develop in these areas, you cannot pass up this book."

Trevor Sullivan, General Manager, DTS International, Sydney, Australia

"Why invest in another book on leadership development? *The Complete Leader* is a remarkable guide for the pilgrim seeking greater clarity about what it takes to become a leader. There are three dimensions that set this read apart: the integrity and wisdom of its authors; the winsomeness of their writing; and the utility and tangible specificity it provides. This book is a gem!"

Nicholas Bauman, President,
Nicholas Bauman & Associates, Inc., Washington D.C.

"Ron and Randy have created an outstanding resource for developing leaders. If you are a coach or a leader who wants to grow, you will value this book as I do."

Shawn Hayashi, Best Selling Author, CEO, The Professional Development
Group LLC, Executive in Residence, Lehigh University MBA

"I highly recommend this book for everyone who thinks what I want my future to be. This great tool gave me a chance to make a journey through myself. Thank you very much, Ron and Randy."

Hasan Tahsin Gungor, Is Kavramlari Danismanlik
Hizmetleri Limited Sirketi, Istanbul, Turkey

"As a former 30 year college coach who was influenced by the leadership of such giants as John Wooden, Vince Lombardi and Bear Bryant, and for the last 15 years learning from the best and coaching in the business world, I can honestly and wholeheartedly say that this book is the compilation of what I call—Coaching the Doctrine of Excellence. Without question, this book will help you build your coaching skills and will benefit you and your team tremendously. The price for success is always paid in advance and this book is a play book of how to put it all together. A must read for all leaders!"

Skip Hall (University of Washington, University of Missouri,
University of Colorado, Boise State University)

"A complete book on *The Complete Leader*! The four dimensional approach to leadership provides an integrated and logical road map for those organizations in search of a working definition of leadership as well as for those aspiring to be leaders or improve on leadership capability. The self assessment (both hand scored and computerized) at the back of the book serves as a comprehensive needs analysis that will be helpful to Executive/Leadership coaches and those planning for leadership training and learning. Nicely done!"

Dr. Shayne Tracy, Master Executive Coach, Toronto, Canada

THE COMPLETE LEADER

EVERYTHING YOU NEED TO BECOME
A HIGH PERFORMING LEADER

RON PRICE AND RANDY LISK

The Complete Leader:
Everything You Need to Become a High-Performing Leader

By Ron Price and Randy Lisk
© 2014 by Price Associates

TriMetrix® is a registered trademark of Target Training International, Ltd.

To purchase copies of *The Complete Leader* in large quantities at wholesale prices, please contact Aloha Publishing at alohapublishing@gmail.com.

Cover design by: Cari Campbell Design
Interior design by: Fusion Creative Works, www.fusioncw.com
Primary Editor: Stacy Ennis

Hardcover ISBN: 978-1-61206-083-5
Softcover ISBN: 978-1-61206-082-8
Casebound Hardcover ISBN: 978-1-61206-255-6

Published by Aloha Publishing

Fourth Printing
Printed in the United States of America

CONTENTS

FOREWORD

BY BILL J. BONNSTETTER

In 1970, I was a college professor teaching management classes to undergraduates in the Midwest. At that time, much of our curriculum was centered on theories by Douglas McGregor of the MIT Sloan School of Management. In particular, Theory X and Y, which addressed perceptions managers held of their employees. Theory X held that ineffective managers were autocratic and believed employees were inherently lazy and disliked and avoided work. Theory Y was more optimistic, positing that effective managers assumed employees were motivated and enjoyed work.

In Theory X, the presence of the manager masked both motivated and lazy workers because people would hide their true nature when the manager was around. Therefore, the manager was dictatorial and controlling. This philosophy of leadership had more to do with controlling people than understanding behavior or values. Unfortunately, many managers subscribe to this type of "leadership."

This theory completely misses what goes on in the workplace—namely, that employees have a variety of personal skills, soft skills and competencies. Today, leaders use knowledge of their employees to advance performance and inspire excellence. Leaders must not only create a vision, but must also engage their teams in that vision. In this way, the team continues to be invested in the vision and spiritedly working toward it, even if the leader is absent.

Recent research I have conducted indicates most leaders have mastered some skills and test above average in many others. I've also found that self-awareness is vital: all leaders must understand what skills they have mastered and what they need to hone, so they can address those weaknesses or hire team members strong in those areas. Understanding their own skill set will additionally help leaders set appropriate and achievable goals and vision. Self-awareness helps them become more effective and always moving forward in the journey toward completeness.

Some of the skills of particular importance for leaders include the ability to create and articulate a vision or goal (a vital part of goal achievement), personal accountability and persuasion. All leaders need a compelling vision. People will not follow someone who doesn't have a vision, a goal—an end in mind. In addition, it's very important for leaders to be personally accountable for their actions. It builds credibility for a leader's team while establishing a culture of integrity for the entire organization. Finally, persuasion is essential to effective leadership. Leaders are continuously called upon to persuade people to appreciate and buy into their visions. All of these skills and more are detailed in *The Complete Leader*, offering leaders both a necessary training tool and lifelong reference guide to help them along their leadership paths.

The difference between a leader and a manager is simple: one leads, while the other controls. In the end, control (and the control-based

Theory X) has little to do with leadership. As a leader, do you control, or do you inspire and lead?

Like Ron and Randy, I believe leadership is a journey, not a destination or a singular achievement. The most important thing to pack on this journey is a desire for continuous learning—about yourself and others. This desire, along with this book, will fuel you as you strive to become a better person and a more complete leader.

PREPARING TO BE A HIGH PERFORMING LEADER

Great leaders do more than just direct those under them. They inspire. They teach. They have a noble calling that extends beyond their office walls—a mission and vision that spreads into the world and influences others for the better.

In our experience coaching executives from small businesses up to Fortune 100 companies, we have met a handful of people who embody excellent leadership. A man named W. James Russell was one such person who impacted Ron's formative years as a young leader. Russell started as a business form salesperson, selling forms out of the trunk of his car. His hard work eventually led to the establishment of a successful business, which received national recognition. But his influence extended beyond sales and profits—his positive impact was felt throughout his entire organization.

Russell's leadership was so wide-reaching that we could spend many pages discussing it. But for our purpose here, there are four characteristics that stand out. First, he was exceptionally clear about what he was trying to accomplish. He often demonstrated his ability to think clearly about strategy by quoting author Peter Drucker. "It's more important to do the right things than to do things right," he would say. He was disciplined at being a clear thinker and holding on to that clarity and focus as the anchor of his business.

The second area he excelled at was managing himself. Russell was a voracious reader, and reading helped him recognize how much energy and time is lost because of a lack of discipline and self-management. He was like a solider when it came to getting things done. He saw that he set the standard for self-management for his whole company, and that he could never demand out of his employees more than he was willing to give himself. He was so developed in that area that it could be both intimidating and inspiring.

The third area he was outstanding in was leading and caring for his team. A lot of times, someone who is so driven and disciplined would have a militaristic approach—more like a general than a leader who wants those under him to grow and succeed as individuals. Yet, Russell was able to see his team as human beings. He set a very high standard for his employees because he believed in them. He valued them but did not use that sentiment as an excuse to not hold them to a high standard. Instead, his care for them was the inspiration to have high standards for their work.

Fourth, and probably most important, Russell was able to develop a unique picture of his ideal self as a one-of-a-kind leader, while still remaining humble. He didn't attempt to mimic anyone else. Instead, he drew from the wisdom and feedback of others to develop a clear picture of his ideal self as a leader. He viewed leading his business as a noble pursuit and saw beyond the extrinsic boundaries to capture an intrinsic motivation through which he changed his world and the worlds of those around him. (For more on his accomplishments and impact, visit www.TheCompleteLeader.org.)

Russell would tell you that he was not a complete leader—but he was a lot more complete than most of us. His example embodies much of what we explore in this book.

THE INCOMPLETE LEADER

What does it mean to be a complete leader? The truth is, there is no such thing. Rather, a "complete leader" is always in the pursuit of completeness. In many ways, a more accurate term would be "incomplete leader," to describe someone who is always expanding his skills and knowledge. As Earl Nightingale said, "Success is the progressive realization of a worthy goal or ideal." He went on to explain that as long as you understand where you are going and you are moving in that direction, you are successful already. Once you achieve your goal, if you do not have another worthy goal or ideal, you cease to be successful. What matters is the process and the journey. The greatest leaders are always striving for more—always working to improve themselves and reach higher. They place importance not just on where they are but also where they have been and where they are going.

Becoming a complete leader is an aspirational vision. Nobody ever crosses the finish line. That is part of the joy—being inspired and compelled and reaching toward completeness. Ultimately, once you have run your leg of the race, you get to pass the baton on to someone else.

Whether you are a CEO of a large corporation or a leader in a smaller company, you are likely reading *The Complete Leader* because you want to become great at what you do. As executive coaches, we help people find their unique talents and possibilities, and then develop and leverage those strengths to increase influence and possibly even change the world. We have designed this book to help you do just that.

The book is divided into twenty-five modules, with each focused on a specific leadership competency. In general, there are five to seven of these competencies that leaders must master, and then everything else falls into place in their leadership. Transformation as a leader compels you to develop your skills to their greatest potential. Doing so opens you up to achieving whatever you set out to do—whether it is an immediate goal like getting promoted or a far-off goal like becoming a top leader in your industry. Research completed by Bill Bonnstetter at TTI Success Insights indicates that five of these modules deserve special attention: personal accountability, persuasion, goal achievement, interpersonal skills and self-management.

This is not a business book in the traditional sense. Rather, it is your gateway to continual learning. Most books offer static information, which can be problematic in today's ever-changing world. To address this, we have created a companion tool at www.TheCompleteLeader.org to further that learning. *The Complete Leader* opens the door to developing yourself, and the website continues that learning through assessments, activities and other methods of applying the skills presented here. (We will discuss the companion site in detail in "1.0 Getting Started.")

Each of the twenty-five competencies was selected based on our individual and shared experiences working with leaders in widely varied fields. The diagnostic tools we use with our clients include skills that unintentionally led to three categories: clear thinking, leading yourself and leading others. We saw that helping leaders understand their talents, and work to develop those talents rather than focus on improving weaknesses, was having an incredible effect. This led us to explore these twenty-five competencies that all leaders should be aware of; what you focus on developing will be unique to your leadership needs. The twenty-five competencies include:

Clear thinking: futuristic thinking, conceptual thinking, planning and organization, creativity, continuous learning, problem-solving, decision-making

Leading yourself: self-management, personal accountability, flexibility, resiliency, goal achievement

Leading others: empathy, understanding and evaluating others, presenting skills, written communication, diplomacy and tact, interpersonal skills, persuasion, negotiation, conflict management, teamwork, employee development and coaching, customer focus

Authenticity: leadership

While writing the content for the modules, we were unexpectedly reinvigorated. When we were partway through, a report came out from the National Academy of Sciences that nearly paralleled the table of contents to *The Complete Leader*. In the 242-page report, the researchers identify three areas of classification for "21st century skills" that impact success: cognitive, intrapersonal and interpersonal. We were excited that their categories were nearly identical to our groupings of clear thinking, managing yourself and leading others, and even more exhilarated as we reviewed the report and found that it reinforced every single concept in this book. It thrilled us to have our work confirmed by such a respected institution.

Since the original publication of this book, TTI Success Insights has continued to evolve their own set of skills. In a majority of instances, this was simply a slight change in the name of the skill with two exceptions: they have added self-starting as a skill for leading yourself, and project management as a skill for leading others. We have chosen not to write about these skills in this latest edition, however readers can find more information on all of the skills and terminology, including the two new ones, at our website TheCompleteLeader.org.

Our backgrounds also played an important role in not only selecting the competencies but also building the content, activities and strategies for each module. Ron has worked in fifteen countries and served in almost every level of executive management over the past thirty-five years. As the former president of a multi-million dollar international company, Ron understands the challenges and risks of running a business and building a dynamic team. He works shoulder-to-shoulder with executive leadership teams to bring strategic clarity and transformational results to organizations—especially those dealing with turmoil and transition. In 2004, Ron started Price Associates, a leadership performance firm that features the bright minds and innovative solutions of some of the world's top consultants in organizational development, process management, branding, marketing and more. He loves helping leaders develop a clear picture of their uniqueness and what is special about their particular talents. He sees *The Complete Leader* and www.TheCompleteLeader.org as his way of helping leaders leverage that uniqueness to create lasting influence.

Randy spent twenty years working as an electrical engineer and product development manager for IBM before becoming an internal consultant focused on market-driven quality. He created and delivered a number of quality and leadership development programs for the IBM division that became Lexmark, and presented these programs to Lexmark's young leaders in the U.S. and seven other countries during the 1990s. He also worked with Stephen R. Covey's organization as a certified facilitator of The 7 Habits of Highly Effective People®. Randy is certified in several additional leadership development programs that he has facilitated over the past twenty years, and he has had a broad impact in multiple industries as a trusted advisor, consultant and coach since leaving his corporate position in 1991 to found Lisk Associates. His son, Ryan, joined the business in January 2007 and took it over in 2011. Randy continues to work with clients part-time, in addition to working on *The Complete Leader* and a number of "retirement projects."

Our decades of experience—both in our own careers and in helping leaders develop theirs—come together in this book. No matter where you are in your leadership, understanding the twenty-five competencies, and focusing closely on developing five to seven of those skills, can have the most powerful impact on your career to date. You can become a great leader, and we will teach you how.

Neither of us claims to be complete leaders. We understand that we are still journeying toward completeness, and we recognize that the leaders we work with are incomplete, too. That is perfectly acceptable—in fact, it is desirable. After all, as we discussed, leadership is a journey, a process, a quest that expands once you reach your destination.

The final test of a leader is his ability to transcend self-interest and self-promotion to serve a greater cause. No leader is ever validated by what they do for themselves; they are validated by what they do for others. *The Complete Leader* is meant to give you the tools to become the greatest version of yourself, and to have a positive impact on others in the process.

1.0

GETTING STARTED

Ever since childhood, most of us are taught to focus on our weaknesses. It starts with repetitive "noes" in the toddler years, progresses to red marks and teacher conferences in school, and becomes the focus of training in college and beyond. With all of this focus on negativity, it can be easy to direct effort and energy to improving those weaknesses. Instead of focusing on developing talents, many people become obsessed with "fixing" the areas they struggle in.

We propose a better way and a more positive approach: focus on your strengths.

That is where *The Complete Leader* comes in. It contains a toolbox of twenty-five of the most important leadership skills that are needed in today's ever-changing work environment. The approach is to explain each skill, help you assess your current capability, and help you develop the competency, if applicable.

Throughout each of the modules, we acknowledge a simple fact: the world is changing. These changes cause a more opaque, uncertain and variable work environment that makes many classic leadership tools and approaches ineffective. While these new realities are important to understand, we will not dwell on them. Instead, our goal is to equip both established leaders and "tomorrow's leaders" with a new mindset and skill set to leverage and address these changes.

TARGET YOUR TRAINING

The Complete Leader approaches leadership development much like an individual coaching session, with a focus on evaluation and then targeted training. The twenty-five skills are divided into four parts, with the full realization that many skills build on, or are related to, others, and that leadership is an integrated whole, not a number of parts.

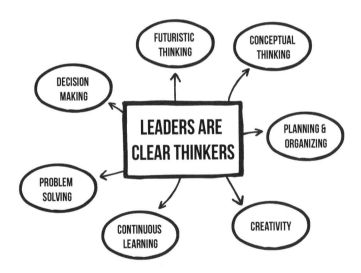

"Part One: Leaders Are Clear Thinkers," deals with thinking skills such as creativity, problem-solving and decision-making. You will find numerous tips and tools to improve your thinking, from futuristic and creative thinking to the more practical areas of planning, decision-making and problem-solving. You will also learn strategies to help you sharpen thinking skills needed by tomorrow's leaders.

"Part Two: Leaders Lead Themselves," deals with skills such as self-management and personal accountability and gives you a road map to improve yourself. Self-improvement does not involve or require others. You simply need to make the necessary choices and practice implementing them in your life and work.

"Part Three: Leaders Lead Others," explains the skills needed to deal effectively with others, such as diplomacy, persuasion and coaching. Covering twelve of the twenty-five leadership competencies, it is the most extensive section, and for good reason. Leadership involves getting things done through the efforts of others, and we explore working with people in detail. You will develop skills to improve your communication, including listening, talking, presenting and writing. The section also focuses on helping you become better prepared to work through any interpersonal situation, including negotiations, managing conflict, working with teams, developing employees and focusing on customers. The lessons in these modules will help you become a better leader.

"Part Four: Leaders Are Authentic," deals with character. Failures as a leader are typically due to one of two issues: problems with competence or problems with character. If tomorrow's leaders wish to be long-term managers, they must have both high integrity and competency in their leadership. The module in this section focuses on developing your character—which extends beyond the workplace and can enhance your personal life, as well.

USING "THE COMPLETE LEADER" STRATEGICALLY

Few people, if any, have fully developed all twenty-five personal skills outlined in this book. Even the best leaders are not good at everything, but they understand their skill sets and work with their strengths while finding ways to neutralize their weaknesses. This list of competencies can serve as a checklist against your own current abilities, and where you want to improve.

The twenty-five skills are explained as short modules, and the book is flexible. While there are several approaches to learning and utilizing the modules, we recommend that you do a cursory read once. As you learn about each of the twenty-five leadership skills discussed in this book, ask yourself, "On a scale of 0-10, 0 being incompetent in a skill and 10 being a role model for this talent, where am I today? Am I happy with this level of competence?" If the answer is "yes," move on to another skill. If not, and if the skill builds on your talents or the needs of your position, ask yourself, "What is my learning strategy?" and "What is my improvement plan?" Keep a list of the competencies you want to work on. We have also provided a self-assessment for each of the twenty-five skills in Appendix 1 to help identify areas of focus. In addition, you will find a description of the leadership profile we use in our work with executive clients in Appendix 2.

After you read the book once, complete the online leadership assessment at the book's companion website, www.TheCompleteLeader.org. Why take an assessment? The only way to see yourself clearly is through feedback. You may be using this book because you have already completed a personal assessment, either the companion assessment to *The Complete Leader* or another, or received feedback from colleagues. If you have not received solicited feedback in a while, we also suggest taking the time to complete an unbiased empirical test and learn from its results. Or, get comments on your current strengths and weaknesses from people who will tell you the truth. Knowing yourself is critical to moving forward in the direction you want to go.

The assessment results and feedback from others will help you identify competencies that you should focus on. Compare that list with the one you made while reading, and select five to seven. It is important to reiterate that no leader can or should focus on developing all twenty-five; trying to focus on too many competencies only draws energy away from the ones that are most important to your leadership. Instead, start with one, and once you have mastered that competency, move to the next.

We also recommend keeping the book on your desk as a necessary reference and resource to help you excel as a leader. One day, if you find you are struggling with organization, for example, you can reference "1.3 Planning and Organization." If you notice that you are consistently not meeting the goals you set, read "2.5 Goal Achievement" and the resources available on the companion website. We designed the book so you can dip back into it as often as you need or want to. This unique "closed-loop" of clear definitions, targeted assessment and a supportive website will give you the best chance of becoming a better leader.

No matter which of the competencies you choose to focus on, "Part Four: Leaders Are Authentic" may be the most important section. The twenty-five competencies are the threads that form the tapestry of leadership, and every leader's tapestry will look different based on his skills and talents. At the heart of great leadership is authenticity, and Part Four is meant to help you understand how to leverage your uniqueness. We recommend reading that section in depth at some point, whether at the beginning of your leadership journey or midway through developing your target competencies. Reread it from time to time, practice the strategies we offer, and be sure to access the additional resources at www.TheCompleteLeader.org.

FOCUS ON DEVELOPING YOUR STRENGTHS

You may wonder why we suggest focusing on just five to seven competencies. Peter Drucker wrote a classic article in a 1999 issue of the *Harvard Business Review* about developing your skills. His article, "Managing Oneself," advocates knowing and developing your strengths. As he says, "It takes more energy to improve from incompetence to mediocrity than to improve from first-rate performance to excellence." It takes receiving feedback—both from others and an honest self-evaluation of your performance—to get this knowledge. Once you understand your strengths and weaknesses, Drucker recommends improving your strengths first, and not getting ensnared by those other talents that you have not developed.

Looking back on his career, Ron sees that he focused too much on improving his weaknesses as a young leader and not enough on developing his natural talents. He took classes, applied discipline and focused most of his professional development on turning his weaknesses into strengths. As a result, he was promoted into roles that used these artificial talents. This approach decreased his overall job satisfaction and took his career in a direction that was not aligned with who he really was. It took him years to unravel this mistake and advance his leadership opportunities around natural talents that he could develop into optimal strengths. Now, he helps others avoid similar mistakes.

CHOOSE WHO YOU WANT TO BE

As you foster your talents, remember that leadership develops from a foundation of who you choose to be. Many of the leadership competencies in this book are choices you can make to *be* a certain kind of leader. For instance, suppose you have chosen to become an empathetic listener—to care about and understand others and hear them as unique humans. Once you identify the type of leader you would like to be, a number of behaviors or things you can *do* become apparent. Just wanting to be empathetic does not work; you have to change certain behaviors to develop into an empathetic listener (see "3.1 Empathy" for a list of these behaviors). And, in the end, you will *have* an empathetic outlook. Empathy is not something you can simply choose to have. You cannot buy it or possess it like you can a new cell phone. It is an effect, not a cause. Behaving with empathy is a result of how well your inside choices are in sync with your outside actions. You have not learned it until you can act empathetically, and do so more or less unconsciously. This takes choice, persistence, feedback and practice.

Leadership develops from *be* to *do* to *have*. It does not run in the other direction. Who do you want to be? The path to leadership competency can be summarized this way:

1. Define who you want to become as a leader.

2. Determine and practice the appropriate behaviors repeatedly.

3. Eventually, you will become the leader you have imagined.

LEARN FROM EXPERIENCE

Think of how a child learns to walk. If you could find someone who had spent all her time in organizations, and none around little kids, she might think, "I bet the child attended a Walking Course for Beginners. Or, at the very least, hired a Walking Coach." Of course, children do neither of those. Although you could say they get some coaching and encouragement from their parents and older siblings, most children learn to walk like we all did. They try something, fall down and then try again. They learn from experience. They get very little instruction and certainly do not read a *Walking for Dummies* manual. They fail, reflect on their failures and learn without being taught. You probably learned to ride a bike or do a number of other things the same way.

Similarly, the way most people learn to do things is through experience. But that is not the way most organizations train and develop their people. Two researchers at the Center for Creative Leadership looked at how adults learn and develop. Their findings resulted in creating a model called the 70-20-10 rule. You may have heard of it because a number of companies have wisely adapted the 70-20-10 rule to guide their employees' development.

The model says that 70 percent of learning comes from real life, on-the-job experiences, tasks and problem-solving—learning by doing. Another 20 percent of learning comes from feedback from others such as coaches, managers and role models. The final 10 percent comes from formal training. This ratio is the opposite of how many companies write their development plans, with courses and reading taking up the 70 percent part and experience counting for 10 percent.

Ron tells of his experience working with one of the great motivational speakers of the twentieth century, Charlie "Tremendous" Jones. While mentoring Ron, their conversation went like this:

"Ron, the key to success as a leader is good judgment," Charlie said.

"But how do you get good judgment?"

"Experience!"

"And how do you get experience?" Ron asked.

"Bad judgment!"

As you read this book and complete the modules, you may want to reflect on the structure of your own educational journey to see if you are being intentional about learning from your experiences. As the saying goes, "You can have ten years' experience or one year's experience ten times." Identify your strengths and what you like to do. Then, have your manager or someone help you take advantage of experiences in the workplace that fit you and enhance your own learning. Enlightened managers understand that developing the capacity and capability of those who work for them is their main job. Information can create knowledge, but it takes a challenge to create experience. Another proven strategy for creating learning experiences is to volunteer for leadership roles in charitable organizations.

LEARN BEYOND EXPERIENCE

Like all models, the 70-20-10 model has its limits. Experience helps us when we face the same or similar situations later. But some decisions involve choices that deal with new situations or subjects, with limited past experience to draw from. As people advance in their careers, they take on more complex challenges that have longer time frames and wider impacts. Strategic decisions may involve several divisions or even several organizations in different parts of the world. Some choices have ramifications that show up years later, such as committing to new technologies, investing in new manufacturing plants and processes, or promoting people into leadership positions.

Because some of these decisions and actions have consequences beyond your learning horizons, experience may be a "learning disability." As Peter Senge says in *The Fifth Discipline*, "Herein lies the core learning dilemma that confronts organizations: we learn best from experience but we never directly experience the consequences of many of our most important decisions."

Even if you do not get to experience the long-term consequences of some of your decisions, you are not off the hook. When a choice needs to be made, it requires a self-aware, thoughtful leader who has developed himself and those around him so that the best possible decision can be made under those circumstances. Abdication is not leadership.

Although the learning beyond experience model does not apply to all decisions, it can help you develop and grow, particularly as you learn to relate to and work with others. Feedback on how you conduct yourself and interact with others is available in the form of helpful facts, data and observations, and is not based on judgment or blame. Now is a good time to honestly evaluate your personal educational strategy. You must take an active role in your learning; it is too important to leave it in the hands of someone else.

BEYOND THE BOOK: A SYSTEM FOR DEVELOPING YOUR LEADERSHIP

The Complete Leader is both a quick-start guide—a way to quickly get you started on your journey—and a necessary reference book that deserves a spot on every leader's desk. But because the ideas presented in these pages are complex and multifaceted, our companion website, www.TheCompleteLeader.org, will help you learn the skills most important to you as a leader and put them into practice. As mentioned, the website includes an assessment that measures your leadership baseline as it directly relates to the twenty-five essential skills discussed in each of the four sections, as well as expands on the modules and concepts. In essence, the website is an expansion of the book—one we are very excited to be able to offer you and your team.

Our approach to leadership is different from others in that we offer a comprehensive, ever-evolving tool specifically suited to your needs as a leader. This combination (book, assessments and website) forms a timeless system that you can use for lifelong leadership development. The twenty-five leadership skills are clearly and specifically defined, and the online assessment measures your competency in each area. The book, improvement plan you develop based on the online assessment, and online resources at www.TheCompleteLeader.org provide a consistent, measurable leadership development system.

If you choose to use this book as a stand-alone entity, we hope it helps you on your leadership path. But to take advantage of our full system, please join our ecosystem of references and conversations around the twenty-five skills at www.TheCompleteLeader.org.

No matter how you use this book, may your journey of growth and development deepen and continue throughout your life. We hope the experience is energizing and rewarding for you, and that *The Complete Leader* enriches your life and the lives of those you lead.

Please visit www.TheCompleteLeader.org for access
to tools, resources, and information.

PART 1:

LEADERS ARE CLEAR THINKERS

As Dr. Stephen R. Covey explained, "Everything is created twice: first in your mind, then in reality." In Part One, we will focus on seven "thinking" skills that help leaders develop mentally so they can see things more clearly. The skills are broken into individual modules:

1.1 Futuristic Thinking – Ability to look beyond present circumstances to see future possibilities

1.2 Conceptual Thinking – Ability to think at an abstract level and apply assumptions to real life

1.3 Planning and Organization – Ability to create and use logical, systematic processes to achieve goals

1.4 Creativity – Ability to combine ideas in new and unique ways to produce a result

1.5 Continuous Learning – Ability and desire to continually gather new knowledge, which is fuel for the brain

1.6 Problem-Solving – Ability to analyze, diagnose and deal with problems effectively

1.7 Decision-Making – Ability to make an informed choice from a number of options

These seven interrelated skills are necessary for leaders to think clearly and make sense out of an increasingly complex world. Without the ability to think clearly, a person can neither lead his own life nor hope to lead others. These are not thinking skills for the sake of an intellectual exercise; they are the foundation for the later talents focusing on doing and relating.

Fully understanding these topics is not possible within the space allowed in this book. That is one reason we created the companion site, www.TheCompleteLeader.org. There, you can explore any of these competencies in greater depth.

FUTURISTIC THINKING

WHAT IS FUTURISTIC THINKING?

Wayne Gretzky, one of the world's greatest hockey players, confessed that he was not the strongest or fastest player when compared to many of his competitors. Instead, he had a natural ability to anticipate where the puck would end up.

Gretzky's observation may sound overly simplistic at first. After all, cannot everyone draw a line from where a puck is to where it is going, based on the direction it is moving? What made Gretzky great was his ability to anticipate several actions that could change the direction of the puck four, five or even eight times, well before they ever happened. He would then head to where the puck would end up. Because others could not anticipate moves as well as Gretzky, he was often the first one there. In this way, Wayne Gretzky was a "futuristic thinker" because he could envision different futures and prepare for them without getting stuck in the present.

Great futuristic thinkers have the ability to imagine, predict and prepare for changes long before other people do. Futuristic thinkers look beyond the current circumstances, assumptions and limitations to anticipate future possibilities. They have the ability to imagine and predict changes that others do not see. They are open to new ideas about their customers, products, services, strategies and even business models. They can exploit opportunities because they are the first to see them coming.

Futuristic thinking is not the same as daydreaming. It is grounded in understanding the present circumstances and a thorough knowledge of your current job or expertise. Futuristic thinkers understand the basics of their industries. They keep an "ear to the ground" for signals about where their industries, markets, customers and competitors are heading (see also "1.5 Continuous Learning"). They marry their understanding of current reality with the ability to see broadly and make connections not obvious to others (see also "1.4 Creativity"). If Gretzky had not understood his game so thoroughly, he could never have envisioned where the puck might go.

WHY IS FUTURISTIC THINKING IMPORTANT?

Tomorrow's leaders will live in a world that changes faster than we have even begun to understand. The word "institution" will become a relic and an anathema to leaders—in many ways, it already has. Knowledge is doubling every thirteen months, with every indication that this rate will continue to increase in the coming decade. Therefore, the half-life of success and competitive advantage is shrinking.

> "The only thing worse than being blind is having sight but no vision."
> – Helen Keller

In order to guide their organizations toward new success, tomorrow's leaders will need to think further into the future, and do it faster and more precisely. No longer will organizations be sustainable by just maintaining success; survival will require creating new successes on a regular basis. Leaders will need to become comfortable with ambiguity and look for opportunities across traditional boundaries, whether geographical, industrial or otherwise.

HOW CAN FUTURISTIC THINKING BE LEARNED?

As with many leadership traits, futuristic thinking is both a talent and a skill. The best futuristic thinkers have a knack for it. No one has to teach them to do it—they naturally look forward. To them, the past is irrelevant and the present is boring. They play mental games, trying to be the first to predict the future. Sometimes, their focus is six months out, and sometimes it is twenty years. Whatever the time frame, they easily anticipate the changes from present realities into future possibilities.

If futuristic thinking comes naturally for you, terrific! Find leadership opportunities where you can develop and apply this talent through practice. You might contribute to the next round of your company's strategic planning or complete your department budget using a future focus instead of extrapolating from the past. Look for chances to utilize your innate ability to think forward.

If futuristic thinking isn't one of your natural talents, you can still develop it as a skill. It will just take more intentional effort. Here are some ways to nurture futuristic thinking:

LISTEN TO AND LEARN FROM OTHER FUTURISTIC THINKERS

Listen attentively to your friends, associates and acquaintances. Do they spend more time talking about the past, the present or the future? Where do they exude the most passion? Just by listening for their dominant orientations, you will begin to identify futuristic thinkers. When you notice someone's passion about the future, start asking questions. The more time you spend with futuristic thinkers, the more you will learn. And since most people are influenced heavily by who they spend time with, over time, you will become more futuristic in your own thinking.

> ## "The best way to predict your future is to create it."
> ## – Abraham Lincoln

READ ARTICLES, BLOGS AND BOOKS BY FUTURISTIC THINKERS

Read materials that focus on future trends, strategy development and growing industries. Even if you do not read all of the content closely, you will begin to think in more future-focused ways. Eventually, you should begin to recognize trends that are echoed by several authors and will likely be drawn to explore how these trends will affect you and your job.

STUDY MAJOR TRENDS IN SOCIETY

What will the future hold in changes to demographics, technology, politics, globalization, and environmental and regulatory issues? Begin researching and studying the trends that directly impact you. Understanding broad, reliable trends in these categories will help you begin developing your own skills to imagine and predict the future.

CONSTRUCT VARIOUS SCENARIOS OR MODELS OF DIFFERENT FUTURES

In the distant past, leaders depended on seers, prophets and crystal balls to help them prepare for an unknown future. The modern equivalent is modeling, usually with the help of computers. Yes, the future is unknown. But if you wait until it arrives, it will be too late to prepare for it. The question is: Can you use models to help your organization prepare for the future, and perhaps avoid some of the most worrisome outcomes?

One type of modeling, known as scenario planning, has been used for a number of years to help people think strategically about the future. In essence, participants construct several different stories or scenarios about how the future might unfold. Typical scenarios include:

- Growth, or Preferred – based on the assumption that the entity in question will thrive

- Collapse, or Doomsday – based on the assumption that the entity will not survive

- Most Likely, or Probable – based on the assumption that the future will unfold as expected

- Transformational, or Utopian – based on the assumption that a major shift will occur that affects the entity

Develop each scenario, and see what unexpected events might show up in these possible futures. Doing so will not only help you foresee the future of the particular scenario in question, but it will also help train you to become a futuristic thinker.

> "The easiest future to envision is your preferred future."
>
> – Glen Hiemstra, author of
> *Turning the Future into Revenue*

BECOME A "FUTURE FICTION" WRITER

Write about the future like an author of historical fiction, but look forward instead of backward. Over time, the discipline of writing will help you imagine and anticipate with greater skill. Choose an area of interest, such as business, sports, entertainment, politics or religion, and begin to write a fictional scenario of how it might change or evolve in the future. Write several paragraphs to tell your story. Then, start again, only this time, imagine a different plot for the same topic. Write four to six unique fictional stories around the same topic, and your futuristic thinking will begin to grow.

> "Everything is created twice: first in your mind,
> then in reality."
> – Dr. Stephen R. Covey

MAKE A LIST OF CHANGES

What has changed in your life over the past decade? List at least twenty things. Then, make a list of how your life, career or business may change over the next decade, once again listing at least 20 changes. For many people, it is easier to think backward, drawing on memory instead of imagination. Starting with your memory helps you recognize how much has changed, and it also makes it easier for you to begin to imagine a different future. We use this exercise often with leadership teams for long-term creative thinking as part of the strategic planning process.

EXERCISE YOUR BRAIN

Play chess or other strategy games that require thinking several steps ahead. The more you do this, the more you wire your brain to think into the future. In fact, new neural pathways can be built by repetitive practice over time.

CONCEPTUAL THINKING

WHAT IS CONCEPTUAL THINKING?

On November 19, 1863, a beleaguered U.S. president stood in the middle of one of the most tragic battlefields in American history, where 172,000 American soldiers had fought each other four and a half months earlier. He was not the main speaker at the event. Facing a probable defeat in the next presidential election because of the nation's distaste for war, he rose and spoke for two minutes. He said:

> Fourscore and seven years ago our fathers brought forth on this continent a new nation, conceived in liberty, and dedicated to the proposition that all men are created equal.
>
> Now we are engaged in a great civil war, testing whether that nation, or any nation, so conceived and so dedicated, can long endure. We are met on a great battlefield of that war. We have come to dedicate a portion of that field as a final resting-place for those who here gave their lives that that nation might live. It is altogether fitting and proper that we should do this.
>
> But, in a larger sense, we cannot dedicate, we cannot consecrate, we cannot hallow this ground. The brave men, living and dead, who

struggled here, have consecrated it, far above our poor power to add
or detract. The world will little note nor long remember what we say
here, but it can never forget what they did here. It is for us the living,
rather, to be dedicated here to the unfinished work which they who
fought here have thus far so nobly advanced. It is rather for us to be
here dedicated to the great task remaining before us—that from these
honored dead we take increased devotion to that cause for which they
gave the last full measure of devotion—that we here highly resolve
that these dead shall not have died in vain, that this nation, under
God, shall have a new birth of freedom, and that government of the
people, by the people, for the people, shall not perish from the earth.

Abraham Lincoln's speech is a moving example of the power of
conceptual thinking. He could have spoken of his generals, particularly because the Union won this battle. He could have focused
on the heroics of soldiers on both sides of the conflict. He could
have criticized his political opponents, choosing to expose their
cowardice and self-interest. Instead, he spoke of a concept that
transcended the ugliness of war—the idea of freedom, demonstrated by a government of, by and for the people. He brought
purpose and meaning to the loss of life by connecting it to the
underlying principles of the nation.

Conceptual thinking is the ability to think at an abstract level: to
consider and apply ideas, principles and assumptions to real-life
circumstances. Like Lincoln, people skilled in conceptual thinking
understand *why* something is being done. They can see through
what is happening to understand the cause. Strong conceptual
thinkers are able to focus on the big picture or directional strategy.
They recognize underlying principles or assumptions that create results. Because they can identify unseen causes and make unobvious
connections, they can easily explain these causes and connections
to others, then apply these underlying insights to create practi-

cal results. Conceptual thinking may be thought of as futuristic thinking applied to present-day problems, because people skilled in conceptual thinking can see past the surface of a situation and understand the underlying theories, models or paradigms that are guiding or creating current results.

> **"If you can dream it, you can do it."**
>
> **– Walt Disney**

People with less-developed conceptual thinking skills will have more trouble understanding concepts such as hierarchy, processes, strategy or any thinking that underlies the behaviors we see every day. These people will attempt to fill in the blanks by inventing reasons why certain things happen, or will be oblivious to certain accepted cultural norms in any organization.

WHY IS CONCEPTUAL THINKING IMPORTANT?

All great individuals, enterprises and nations are built upon strong conceptual thinking. This well-known quote from the Declaration of Independence provided the foundation for a great nation:

> We hold these truths to be self-evident, that all men are created equal, that they are endowed by their Creator with certain unalienable Rights, that among these are Life, Liberty and the pursuit of Happiness.

Concepts are the containers for future realities. They can be "grand" ideas, principles that guide actions, heuristics (rules that are loosely defined), or models used to interpret and understand practical situations. In the groundbreaking book, *The Structure of Scientific Revolutions*, Thomas Kuhn showed that science does not advance in an orderly fashion toward greater discoveries but remains fixed in a particular explanation or paradigm until a set of problems is not effectively solved by those assumptions. For example, a paradigm shift occurred when the belief (fact) that the world was flat was replaced by the discovery (fact) that the world was round. Prior to this discovery, the known world was limited by boundaries of fear and ignorance. With the new paradigm, a new world opened up (though it wasn't new, it was always there) and exploration expanded rapidly, creating a multitude of opportunities for our ancestors. Without this new paradigm, it is reasonable to assume that most of us would never have come into existence.

When anomalies arise in accepted thinking, we are forced to change the way we see reality. With great difficulty, a new paradigm emerges to resolve the new problems. As Einstein said, "We cannot solve our problems with the same level of thinking that created them."

Sometimes imaginative new concepts result in products that cause paradigms to shift. Such a shift occurred when a telephone changed from being an appliance that sat on a desk to a multipurpose computer that is carried in a pocket. Now, most people cannot imagine a world without smartphones. Strong conceptual thinkers are able to bring to light ideas that are normally hidden and implicit, well before others recognize those ideas.

"Whatever you can vividly imagine, ardently desire, sincerely believe, and enthusiastically act upon, must inevitably come to pass."

– Napoleon Hill

The way people think—the prevailing paradigms—can also impact every aspect of the success of a company. You have probably heard the idea that "people create an organization." People's conscious and unconscious beliefs about an organization impact processes, culture, behaviors and results, among other functions. Conceptual thinkers are able to identify what drives people to help explain why the company is performing as it is.

Dr. Peter Senge popularized the term "system thinking" as the process of understanding how elements of a system influence one another (see Image 1-1). System thinkers refer to "four levels of system thinking which build on each other." The first or most obvious level is *results*. Everyone can see results. The second level, *behavior*, is what produces results; most people can identify behaviors. The third level, known as *structures*, is all the things that influence behavior. Structures are less obvious and include such things as organization charts, rules, policies and informal procedures. The deepest level, the fourth level, is the *conceptual* level. This level includes the concepts, models, beliefs and assumptions of the leaders.

FOUR LEVELS OF A SYSTEMS VIEW [1]

LEVEL 1. EVENTS

Results, headlines, real happenings which we observe
Conclusions stated as facts "The problem is..."

LEVEL 2. PATTERNS OF BEHAVIOR

Events, behaviors or variables that change over time
The system's "memory."

LEVEL 3. STRUCTURES

Cause and effect relationships between variables
procedures, laws, reporting relationships, usually "things"
Event generators

LEVEL 4. MENTAL MODELS

Internal thinking, assumptions, beliefs
"The way the world is"
The reason for the structure

---

1 Ref. The Fifth Discipline Fieldbook pgs 97-112

The beliefs of the leaders create an organization's structure. The structure influences the behavior that creates the results. It is all connected, and it all starts with you, the leader. An organization's results begin with, and flow from, the beliefs, paradigms or "mental models" of its leaders. If you want to create systemic change, the highest leverage occurs at the conceptual level.

> "Every institution has to organize systematic innovation, that is, create the different tomorrow that makes obsolete and, to a large extent, replaces even the most successful products of today in an organization."
>
> – Peter Drucker

Tomorrow's leaders will need to think conceptually across all boundaries (customers, products, markets, demographics, cultures, geographies, maybe even planets) to survive. Competition will emerge from someone not currently in their field, with great surprise to the current market leaders. Many business models and expertise will have a shelf life of five years or less.

HOW IS CONCEPTUAL THINKING LEARNED?

Great conceptual thinkers appreciate the value in paradoxes, metaphors, paradigms and mysteries. Their attitude is, "As long as this concept is helpful, we will use it. When it breaks down and doesn't solve problems or guide meaningful direction, we will abandon it." Almost unconsciously, they create new concepts by blending mental models, principles, heuristics and assumptions.

Conceptual thinking is easy for some leaders. This skill allows them to enjoy conversations about business philosophy, strategy and vision. For others, developing conceptual thinking skills requires effort. If the latter applies to you, here are some ways to increase your skills in conceptual thinking:

PRACTICE FUTURISTIC THINKING

Practicing the futuristic thinking suggestions in module 1.1 will also strengthen your conceptual thinking.

STUDY STRATEGIES

Study an effective strategy in life, business or government to identify the underlying concepts that made it successful. Do the same with an ineffective strategy, also. For example: When Ronald Reagan spoke in Berlin, he said, "Mr. Gorbachev"—who was not present— "tear down this wall." Reagan was talking about more than the physical wall; he was not asking Gorbachev to call in a demolition crew. Instead, he was appealing to the concept of freedom through a metaphor, urging Gorbachev to recognize the failures of the Soviet concepts of government control, central planning and collectivism. Some people ridiculed him for useless rhetoric. Several German leaders have since said that his statement and the concepts behind it were the catalyst for the fall of the Soviet Union. Reagan's strategy was to engage the minds and hearts of the German people at a conceptual level through his theatrical dialogue with Gorbachev.

IDENTIFY UNDERLYING ASSUMPTIONS IN YOUR ORGANIZATION'S STRATEGY

Step back from your day-to-day work and take a deep look at your organization's strategy. Which of the strategy assumptions are likely to still be relevant in 20 years? Which will become obsolete? Which have already become obsolete? What does your strategy assume about the world, your organization and your competitors? For instance, how will changing demographics impact the underlying strategies in your business? How will the evolution of the Internet or globalization impact your future direction? How will you leverage these changes? How might they threaten you?

IDENTIFY UNDERLYING ASSUMPTIONS BEHIND YOUR ORGANIZATION'S STRUCTURE

Many other unseen factors make up the structure for a particular workplace: hierarchy within the organization, locations of various functions (such as marketing, accounting and so on), ways of getting things done, and other factors such as unofficial rules and procedures. How does this affect work within your organization, either positively or negatively? When thinking conceptually, it is also helpful to clarify the "why"; after all, understanding the "why" is the base of conceptual thinking. Once it is clear why something is occurring, the "how" will come more easily. Why is the organization what it is today? Which assumptions about such things as processes, rules and people are helpful, and which have become obstacles to success?

LOOK FOR CONCEPTS

Identify and analyze models, concepts and principles operating in the world around you to determine which ones are useful and which ones are irrelevant or harmful. For example, with so much globalization of consumer goods and multi-national companies, is it useful, irrelevant or harmful to label products based on national boundaries, such as "Made in China"?

Industrial statistician George Box noted that "all models are wrong...and some are useful." Conceptual thinking is not meant to be precise. Instead, it is directional, helping people understand the big picture. It also helps provide leaders with general guidance for how to respond when varied results arise as they implement their vision.

PLANNING AND ORGANIZATION

WHAT ARE PLANNING AND ORGANIZATION?

Randy's dad was an architectural engineer and a home builder who designed and built custom homes. Before he started building, he planned and organized each project to suit the owner, both aesthetically and financially. He worked in the days before computer-aided design, drawing all his plans by hand, so the process was much slower than it is today. After the client approved the plans, he hired subcontractors who were able to complete the house with all the amenities and within the costs he had estimated. Otherwise, there would be no profit. Without planning and organization, he would have failed.

Ever since childhood, every time Randy began a project, no matter how small, his dad always asked him if he had created a plan to achieve it. A person with a plan knows how he is going to get where he needs to go.

Planning and organization is the ability to create and use logical, systematic processes to achieve goals. A person who is skilled in planning and organization creates a desired objective in her mind.

She then visualizes the steps needed to reach the objective, well before the steps actually occur. Her mind naturally organizes each step needed to reach the goal, and she documents the process so it can be used by others. Finally, she uses the created process as a road map to complete a project, modifying it when faced with new information that affects her plan. Some people are so adept at this skill that it becomes the central part of their careers; many become certified project management professionals.

> ## "Measure twice, cut once."
> ### – Proverb

A person who has not yet developed planning and organization skills will tend to "shoot from the hip" and "hope for the best." When given a new project, she may either jump in without thinking it through or procrastinate because she cannot see the way forward. If the project hits a roadblock, she will have trouble figuring out how to modify her original approach. Poorly planned projects waste resources, frustrate people and lower the chance for successful completion. If you are not a natural planner or organizer, there are ways to develop this skill detailed later in this module.

WHY ARE PLANNING AND ORGANIZATION IMPORTANT?

The world today is full of people who are more interdependent yet more geographically dispersed. Diverse teams of people located around the globe may create information that exists only in a software cloud. Working successfully in this manner is not a solitary event. The glue that holds this type of project together is a clear and complete plan, backed up by involved project managers who keep the various pieces working together in sync. And that does not just apply to working virtually. Even people within the same building need clear objectives and a plan for everyone to follow, or success will be hard to come by.

Without a plan, there is no accountability. In "2.2 Personal Accountability," we point out that "[it] is impossible to be accountable for something until you are clear about what it is." Effective leaders help keep their team members accountable by creating workable plans, so that everyone knows what is expected prior to beginning the challenge.

Planning and organization also help leaders communicate effectively. The plan and its potential changes must be communicated to and understood by the team if a project is to be successful; this is especially critical with diverse and dispersed groups. An effective plan helps everyone concentrate on both important objectives and overall goals, and identifies due dates and what tasks need to be delegated.

> **"The main thing is to keep the main thing the main thing!"**
>
> **– Dr. Stephen R. Covey**

HOW ARE PLANNING AND ORGANIZATION LEARNED?

PLAN-DO-CHECK-ACT

Understanding the Plan-Do-Check-Act (PDCA) process is the most important first step to developing planning and organization skills. This process is the cycle of scientific achievement and learning, first explained by Walter Shewhart in his 1939 book on crop mutation. American statistician Dr. W. Edwards Deming learned the timeless concept from Shewhart and utilized it with the Japanese after WWII to improve the quality of their products. Countless companies across the globe use some version of PDCA today to improve processes and products. Having a grasp of the process is necessary for planning and organizing in any setting (see Image 1-2).

PLAN·DO·CHECK·ACT IMPROVEMENT CYCLE

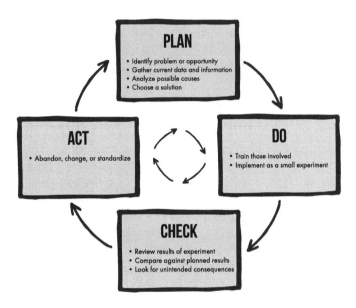

PLAN
- Identify problem or opportunity
- Gather current data and information
- Analyze possible causes
- Choose a solution

DO
- Train those involved
- Implement as a small experiment

CHECK
- Review results of experiment
- Compare against planned results
- Look for unintended consequences

ACT
- Abandon, change, or standardize

MAKE PLANNING AND ORGANIZING A PRIORITY

There is an old line that says, "When you want it bad, you get it bad." Doing things quickly may be useful in the short term. However, doing things quickly and poorly is false progress because you often have to do them over again. Planning and organizing at the outset of a project may seem like more work, but it almost always saves time and energy—not to mention stress and missed deadlines—in the long run. Make a pact with yourself that you will resist the temptation to start a project before you have a workable plan to get to the finish line.

Ron's friend once shared a story about one of his commanders in the Air Force. The commander would ask his subordinates for "vector checks"—regular updates on their projects—to make sure they were not "all thrust and no heading." Ron's friend says that, to this day, he always "sets and rechecks his heading" before putting energy into a project.

SELECT APPROPRIATE TOOLS

There are many different ways to organize, from a simple decision tree to complex software-driven programs. If you are baking a cake, using a recipe—a simple checklist with a list of ingredients and a few instructions—will be sufficient. If you are building the next great airliner, you will need more than a checklist. Make sure the tool you choose fits the project. But ensure that it is not so complex that the tool *becomes* the project; it should support and help you and your team, not hinder progress.

> **"Failing to plan is planning to fail."**
> **– Alan Lakein**

Everyone needs a few simple, reliable tools for planning and getting organized, even if it is just to keep track of a daily or weekly schedule. The best way to create the future you want is to begin planning it today. To borrow from Habit 2 of Dr. Stephen R. Covey's *The 7 Habits of Highly Effective People*, you should "Begin with the End in Mind." How deep you go with your planning tools should be determined by what you want to accomplish, how much planning you want to do yourself, and how much planning you choose to delegate. You may want to pick up some planning software and learn how to use it, or you might even choose to become an expert: a certified project management professional.

Here are some methods of planning and organizing that might work for your organization or project:

Quarterly, Annual and Longer Planning. To run the marathon of life, it is important to start with "why." This means that you develop a deep sense of what is important to you, something that makes life worth living—this applies in business, too! When you have a clear, strong, compelling "why," the "how" and "what" are much easier to understand and organize. "How" and "what" are created through daily, weekly and monthly planning (detailed later in this module).

Strategic Planning. Long-range planning is applicable at both the individual and organizational level; strategic planning is long-range planning applied to the organization. It is part of every leader's job to clarify and communicate answers to two basic questions: "Where are we going?" and "What are we doing?" Strategic planning helps answer those questions.

As with an individual, this type of organizational planning requires clarifying what is important to the organization. This is usually documented in vision and mission statements. The planning work that follows can take a number of forms, including one well-known approach known as a SLOT (Strengths, Limitations, Opportunities, Threats) analysis. A SLOT analysis can be done with or without a facilitator, depending on the development level of the group. It looks at:

- **Strengths**: What are our internal strengths? What are we known for? What do we do best?

- **Limitations**: Where are we vulnerable? If we were our competitors, where would we attack our own organization? (We refer to these as "limitations" instead of the more traditional "weaknesses" because, until you know your strategy, you don't know whether these are areas of vulnerability.)

- **Opportunities**: What is happening outside of our organization that we can take advantage of?

- **Threats**: What is happening outside of our organization that could harm us?

The results of this analysis become the starting point for the strategic plan. For more on approaches to strategic planning, visit our website at www.TheCompleteLeader.org.

Monthly Planning. Monthly goals can connect you to the big ideas in your career, business and life. To make your goals more potent, think about making them SMART. This means they are:

- **Specific**: At this level of planning, the conceptual is not enough. Get as specific and detailed as possible. Each goal should answer the five "W" questions: who, what, where, when and why.

- **Measurable**: Set objective measures that will make it obvious whether you did or did not achieve the goal. Do not leave any wiggle room. The goal should answer the questions: How much? How many? When will I know it is accomplished?

- **Achievable**: Make sure each goal is achievable. Some people need to make fewer commitments and have better execution, while others need to push themselves to be more aggressive in order to achieve the larger results they desire. It is okay to set "stretch" goals, but aim for setting monthly goals that have at least a 75-percent probability of being achieved.

- **Relevant**: Your goals should matter to you, your team, your family or your organization. They should be worth your time and effort. Make sure your goals do not compromise or dilute your vision, mission and long-term direction.

- **Time-bound**: Set specific, non-negotiable deadlines. A goal should include a target date, or a "by when" statement. Once again, aim to achieve your deadlines 75 percent of the time or better.

Weekly Planning. Organize your week by scheduling the most important activities first, providing generous time to focus on your priorities. Next, fill in your calendar with those activities of lesser importance. This will help you develop the habit of doing "first things first." Ron labels all goals, tasks and appointments as:

A = critical to survival

B = important to long-term success

C = some limited importance (including short-term)

D = no or unknown importance

Then, he numbers all of the A priorities by relative importance (ex. A1, A2, A3, etc.) and so on with his B and C goals, tasks and appointments.

GOALS:

A1: Complete our strategic plan for 2014 – 2016 by 12/1/2013

A2: Complete our 2014 financial management plan by 12/30/2013

B1: Review and commit to new CRM with team by 11/30/13

B2: Develop/confirm individual business plan for 2014 with Andy Johnson by 12/19/2013

B3: Create program around "Managing Change" by the end of Q4 2013

B4: Develop recruiting plan for Q2 2014 by 2/28/2014

C1: Create new content for "Effective Non-Profit Boards" by end of Q1 2014

C2: Create a notebook of all past programs delivered over the past 3 years

APPOINTMENTS:

A1: Pam/dinner, 11/3/13 @ 6 pm

A2: Tax attorney, 11/4/13 @ 2 pm

A3: Bill Bonnstetter, 11/4/13 @ 4:30 pm (phone)

B1: Skip Hall, 11/5/13 @ 8:30 am

*B2: Tim Eckstrom, 11/5/13 @ 11 am

B3: Sharon Brooks, 11/5/13 @ 2 pm

B4: NNU Business Advisory Group meeting, 11/6/13 @ 12 noon

C1: Haircut, 11/6/13 @ 10 am

TASKS:

B1: Call Lucas

*B2: Respond to Bryan's e-mail about strategic planning retreat

*B3: Follow up with Rick Smith about next steps

B4: Read for 30 minutes: "Antifragile"

B5: Exercise for 30 minutes

C1: Check new apps for task management

C2: Clean up e-mail folders

C3: Pick up dry cleaning

C4: Re-organize Dropbox files

Daily Planning. Daily planning helps you be more productive. Every day, write your tasks down. Keep the list short (realistic), and prioritize the tasks, starting with 1, then 2, and so on. Place an asterisk (*) next to any task that is urgent, meaning it *must* be completed before the end of the day. As much as possible, start with priority number 1 and complete it before starting on number 2. Some days, you will not complete every task on your list, but at least you will address them with clarity of importance and, when appropriate, the right sense of urgency.

An example of a SMART goal would be, "I will lose six pounds within twelve weeks by changing my diet and exercise habits in order to be healthier and more productive." A "DUMB" goal would be to "try to lose some weight."

DO NOT ASSUME YOU KNOW IT ALL

Planning and organization in an ever-changing world must include built-in flexibility, incorporating the ideas of volatility and uncertainty. As you review your plan, cast a broad net around what might happen. Create a plan that is robust enough to respond to the unknown, and be flexible enough to revise it, when needed. Hope for the best but plan for the worst. Even then, you cannot predict everything. When the unexpected happens, the antidote is to be able to recognize it and respond quickly (see "2.3 Flexibility"). Do not fall in love with your plan to the exclusion of testing it against reality. This is where the "check" part of the Plan-Do-Check-Act process comes in. Continue to check your plan as it progresses.

1.4

CREATIVITY

WHAT IS CREATIVITY?

Ron heard a story years ago about a semi-truck getting stuck under a bridge because its trailer was too tall. The truck would not go forward or backward, having been wedged tightly into the underside of the bridge. Police and firemen huddled with the driver, trying to come up with a way to free the trailer. As they considered and rejected idea after idea, a nine-year-old boy approached the huddle and asked what they were doing. One of the officers explained the predicament to the boy with a condescending tone, as if to say, "We are busy doing grown-up work, so leave us alone." The boy watched them argue for a few minutes and then piped up, "Why don't you just let the air out of the tires?"

Creativity is the ability to think in new ways. It involves going beyond traditional ideas, rules and methods to express something differently or solve a problem. Being creative starts with a need, problem or opportunity and may arise from internal or external prompting. For example, a need may come from someone's emotions, such as a need to express oneself through painting, or from a need to solve a puzzle, such as figuring out why an apple falls from a tree. The impetus for creativity may also come from a perceived opportunity, or a desire to help, such as a decision to develop a cure for polio.

There are two types of creativity: compositional and improvisational. Compositional creativity, which was first proposed by Graham Wallas' in his book, *The Art of Thought*, is creating new products through careful planning, supported by a strict stage-gate process. There are typically four stages to compositional creativity—preparation, incubation, illumination and verification—which make up the typical creativity process in most mature organizations. Improvisational creativity is a more dynamic, spontaneous creativity typically evoked by an immediate need for a response. The difference between the two kinds of creativity is the amount of time available to react. Improvisational creativity mainly relies on intuition, often as a result of well-learned routines that are developed prior to the emergence of the crises or opportunity.

WHY IS CREATIVITY IMPORTANT?

The parade route for the march of civilization is paved by creativity. Organizations must innovate and adapt to survive and thrive, and creativity unlocks innovation and adaptation and allows new ideas to flourish. Leaders have always been using creative ideas to change the world. What is different for tomorrow's leaders is that the pace of change is making the life span of a creative idea shorter. New ideas are needed more frequently for an organization to stay competitive, which prompts the need to have creative people in your organization. The growth of creative industries worldwide continues to signify the rising demand for creative people, or "designers," in business. These designers systematically transform ideas into reality using creative problem-solving capabilities to address a particular challenge in a new way. The creative process also brings convergence between technical and market knowledge, thus increasing potential economic value of the final product. Therefore, design strategy, as an expression of creativity, is critical for future growth for any organization.

> "Imagination is everything. It is the preview
> of life's coming attractions."
>
> – Albert Einstein

Also, improved communication has opened up a much bigger playing field in which to find new ideas. Excellence in one industry is often superseded by an idea from a totally unrelated field. In the past, groups of people located close to each other would tinker with an idea and continue to improve it. Now, the people who make up such groups may be located anywhere in the world, and may be working in a different field.

In his book, *The Innovator's Dilemma*, Harvard's Clayton Christensen describes how industries and markets are being disrupted and overthrown by creative new products and business models. He calls this radical change "creative destruction." Examples of creative destruction abound. The music industry moved quickly from vinyl to discs to online music. Telecommunications changed from party lines to cordless to wireless to Voice Over Internet Protocol (VOIP). Is your phone also a music device or a telecommunications device? How about a camera?

Creative destruction results in new markets and new market leaders. Paradoxically, companies at the top of their industry, with the largest market share and the greatest number of resources, are the most vulnerable to becoming irrelevant—overtaken by the industrial equivalent of a nine-year-old child. The survival mantra is "innovate or die."

In the future, leaders will need the skills and desire to nurture, study and affirm the creativity of all employees, suppliers, customers and sometimes even competitors. Leaders will need to think in networks of creativity rather than in companies, departments or single geniuses. It is important to note that the creative process does not always result in new products and actions, as the success of products or actions also depend on other market conditions and appropriateness. However, if there is no creativity, it is guaranteed that the market movement will cause the organization to fail over time.

HOW IS CREATIVITY LEARNED?

DO NOT RUSH TO JUDGMENT

Sadly, one of the most common statements we hear from leaders is, "I am not very creative." Our experience does not bear this out. We have seen over and over again that everyone can be creative. Everybody has an imagination. Everybody has knowledge. All you need to combine knowledge with imagination is a little patience and confidence. People tend to judge initial ideas too soon and, as a result, limit the breadth of ideas that would otherwise emerge. Just let your imagination go, and collect as many ideas as possible. Include all ideas, especially the "crazy" ones.

> "All good ideas are terrible until people realize they are obvious. If you're not willing to live through the terrible stage, you'll never get to the obvious part."
>
> – Seth Godin

This confidence is particularly critical when creating new products that take thousands of additional ideas to make the "main original" idea possible and valuable to execute. For instance, if you want to manufacture a special coffee mug for geeks, it will take more than just the idea of the cup to know how to design the product. You must consider creative alternatives about materials, colors, manufacturing, market testing and much more. It is during the synthesis of all the crazy, seemingly disruptive ideas that you find the excellent options, or at least combine some of the ideas so you can find the best ones. Indeed, one of the greatest ways to become more creative is through looking at things that do not necessarily fit your original vision and assessing how those ideas can be made applicable in your context.

> "Around here, however, we don't look backwards for very long. We keep moving forward, opening up new doors and doing new things, because we're curious... and curiosity keeps leading us down new paths."
> – Walt Disney

BEWARE OF THE CURSE OF KNOWLEDGE

In their book, *Made to Stick*, the Heath brothers coined the term "The Curse of Knowledge." They explain that knowledge can be a curse and barrier to creativity. People often get moved into leadership roles because they have demonstrated an ability to accomplish things. They have knowledge. Knowledge is helpful; nobody wants someone who is incompetent to lead the charge. But sometimes that person begins to see himself as the expert and believes his knowledge is the one and only way to think. If that happens, it may become difficult for him to think in new and creative ways, like he did when he was a "beginner." He automatically goes to his memory, and when he recalls an idea that has worked in the past, he quits thinking and starts implementing. At that point, he has the curse of knowledge.

The Curse of Knowledge
Ref: Made To Stick by the Heath Brothers

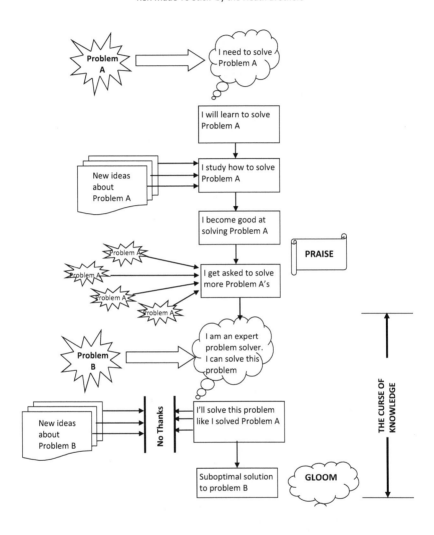

As Shunryu Suzuki writes in the beginning of his book, *Zen Mind, Beginner's Mind*, "In the beginner's mind there are many possibilities, but in the expert's mind there are few." An experienced leader is not a bad thing, and ideas that worked in the past may still be useful in the future. But experience should not block creativity.

Instead, use the experience to create innovative ways to solve problems and encourage new thinking.

> **"He who is good with a hammer thinks everything is a nail."**
>
> **– Abraham Maslow**

EXPAND POSSIBILITIES

Creativity takes a beginner's mind, an explorer's curiosity, and a willingness to suspend judgment or "not know" for a while. The creative process begins by becoming more aware of the world around you, particularly outside your chosen field. Remember: your competition will likely come from an unexpected place. Steve Jobs traveled to Europe early in his career, observing the design of products that had nothing to do with computers. As a result, the clean lines of an early Macintosh computer had their genesis in the clean lines of a Cuisinart kitchen appliance.

In the beginning of a project, creative people try to generate and collect as many ideas as possible, withholding judgment about their quality. As a simple example, think about bricks. Bricks are used to build buildings. Give yourself a couple of minutes to think about all the other possible uses for a brick. You will soon realize that bricks can do much more than form the outside of buildings. Being able to look at a familiar article or situation in a new and different way is one key to creativity.

COMBINE IDEAS IN NEW WAYS

Thomas Edison, holder of 1,093 U.S. patents, grew plants and experimented until he found one that would work as the filament for the first practical incandescent bulb. He finally used carbonized bamboo, an idea that came to him as he was observing the bamboo filaments on his fishing pole. He saw something ordinary and found a different use for it, and the combination changed the world.

> "The chief enemy of creativity is good sense."
> – Pablo Picasso

Luckily, you do not need to be the world's greatest inventor to combine ideas in new ways. Open your mind, collect a lot of options and suspend judgment. Let them "percolate" in your subconscious. A new idea may show up unannounced when you are showering or taking a walk. Try to look at your particular problem with fresh eyes and a beginner's mind. A beginner does not know what will not work or what has already been tried. Withhold judgment for now; judgment comes later. Edison said that many of life's failures come from people who did not realize how close they were to success when they gave up. In most cases, they quit prematurely because of engaging judgment too early in the creative process.

SEEK APPROPRIATE HELP

As a leader, one of your jobs is to decide how much outside help you need to be able to create something new. Sometimes "crowdsourcing," or putting your problem out to the masses, can lead to new ideas. If you try crowdsourcing, you will get several ideas; some will be useful, and others will not. You will still need to filter through all the ideas to decide which ones to consider.

You may not want to be that open or public about your problem or opportunity. If this is the case, you can still invite a small group of people to help with the ideas. This "invitation only" approach provides you more control, but you may miss connecting with someone from another industry who can give you the most help.

If you want help from others, remember that creative solutions rarely come from someone who claims to have solved a problem identical to yours. On the other hand, it is likely that your problem is not completely unique, and there may be similar problems in other industries. Perhaps your answer lies in an idea you can adapt from an unrelated industry. There is no one answer to the question of how much outside help to seek. Just be thoughtful about your decision.

"It's not what you look at that matters, it's what you see."

– Henry David Thoreau, *Walden*

We cover the implementing phase of Creativity in "1.6 Problem-Solving," "1.7 Decision-Making" and in Part 2, "Leaders Lead Themselves."

CONTINUOUS LEARNING

WHAT IS CONTINUOUS LEARNING?

Ron worked with the CEO of a health care system who continually challenged his executive team with new concepts, practices and projects. He stayed abreast of what was new in his profession by studying the thought leaders in health care. In Ron's personal interviews with members of the CEO's team and board of directors, the CEO was consistently praised for his future-oriented leadership—a trait that came naturally from his commitment to continuous learning.

Continuous learning is the knowledge, skills and attitude needed to create an ongoing personal process of learning and development. People who are skilled in continuous learning naturally take the initiative to learn and implement new ideas and methods. These people are often described as "lifelong learners." They find ways to learn about their interests and the work they are engaged in.

Being a continuous learner has both a personal and an organizational component. Some individuals are inherently more interested in learning than others, and some organizations create learning environments as part of their organizational DNA. Continuous learning reflects a desire to keep getting better, an awareness that there is always much more to know, and a practical commitment to increasing competence.

One of Ron's colleagues provides thirty minutes of paid time every day for each of his several hundred employees to read from a recommended list of personal and professional development books. Once a quarter, each employee devotes a full day to what he refers to as "extended reading." His own experience taught him that these intense times of dedicated learning open up unique depths of insight and mental conditioning in the individual. He believes his focus on continuous learning for every employee represents an investment, not a cost; as such, he credits this practice as one of the key components of his long-term business success.

WHY IS CONTINUOUS LEARNING IMPORTANT?

The U.S. Army coined the acronym "VUCA" a number of years ago. It stands for Vulnerability, Uncertainty, Complexity and Ambiguity, and it describes our ever-changing environment. We live in an interconnected world—interconnected to the point of complexity, ambiguity and uncertainty. Many of the methods developed to deal with yesterday's problems assumed defined solutions, based on a set of well-understood causes and effects. But these methods are not sufficient in a VUCA world. People who thrive in this somewhat chaotic world do so by thinking in novel ways and exploring new solutions. Few leaders will progress or thrive by repeating the same behaviors and holding the same beliefs for years on end. Continuous learning counteracts VUCA because it provides a constant stream of fresh knowledge and ideas to help leaders deal with the new problems and ambiguity.

> "In a time of drastic change it is the learners who inherit the future."
>
> – Eric Hoffer

While individuals need to be continuous learners to succeed, entire organizations must also embrace this skill. Tomorrow's leaders—the people who will establish an organization's culture—must embrace continuous learning as both a personal and an organizational value. Organizations will need to invest in knowledge-sharing structures and tools to encourage learning. As a leader, you want your employees to be able to lay their hands on the answer to their question immediately, without taking hours to try to find it. This requires a learning environment where knowledge is captured and easily available, regardless of whether the knowledge resides in the office nearby or halfway around the world.

Continuous learning is no longer the responsibility of the human resources department, although it can be a strong supporter of the concept. Tomorrow's leaders will embrace the idea of learning and knowledge-sharing across the widest boundaries. Not only will they know that success involves "getting more brains in the game," but they will be met with many opportunities and modalities to learn and involve others. Learning is more the responsibility of the learner, whether an individual or a team, and less the responsibility of the organization. Eventually, learning will not be a separate activity or considered "not real work"; instead, continuous learning will be an integral part of any job and captured learning will be an increasingly valuable intangible asset. Learning will not be measured by classroom hours but by results in the marketplace.

HOW IS CONTINUOUS LEARNING LEARNED?

MAKE THE CHOICE

First and foremost, you must make a personal choice to become a continuous learner. Ask yourself this question: Did your education end at graduation, or was that when it really started? If you are intrinsically motivated by learning, you are probably a natural learner. You may have been inquisitive and curious since you were a child, solving puzzles and learning new things.

To develop this skill further, you need to make the choice to *be* a continuous learner. Then, the appropriate things you need to *do* will become more evident.

Think about what you, as a continuous learner, will do. You will be looking for learning that supports your passions and goals. If you are not naturally motivated in this way, you can increase your intrinsic motivation by connecting continuous learning to your passions.

IDENTIFY YOUR PASSIONS

One way to encourage continuous learning is to identify your passions. For example, if you have a passion for making money, consider whether you could make more money if you had additional learning. Perhaps money is not your top motivator. If you are interested in being creative, follow that natural path. Learn more about creativity, art, architecture, photography or whatever interests you. Learning will enhance your creativity. If you are passionate about helping others, learn more about volunteering, philanthropy or other ways to help mankind.

MENTALLY CREATE YOUR FUTURE

Take the time to think about your passions and "stretch" goals. If you could wave a magic wand, what would you become? If you stretched or pushed yourself to become what you really wanted to become, what would you need to learn? Refer to the previous module, "1.4 Creativity," during this exercise, if it helps.

Now, imagine yourself at the end of your life. What do you want to have accomplished, or what would you want people to say about you? Use your imagination, not your memory. Consider all the key roles in your life: work, family, community, spiritual and social. This exercise, if done thoughtfully and then repeated over time, will offer up many avenues for learning and exploration.

BE CONSISTENT AND PERSISTENT

Lay out your learning path so that, over a few years, you will feel like you have become an "expert" in your field. Notice the word "continuous" in continuous learning.

> **"Never become so much of an expert that you stop gaining expertise. View life as a continuous learning experience."**
>
> **– Denis Waitley**

Ron schedules thirty minutes a day, every day, for reading. He says this discipline has helped his career more than any other activity. Be intentional. Make learning a priority in your life and on your schedule. Find out who the giants are in your areas of interest, and begin by reading or listening to some of their thoughts. Follow them anywhere they share their ideas through social media.

EARN A PHD

Ron teaches audiences the concept of earning a new PhD every three to five years. He explains that any credible PhD program has three phases: First, you study the thought leaders and best practices in a specific discipline or science. Next, you advance knowledge in this field of expertise by creating a dissertation. Finally, you submit your findings to a group of peers for critical analysis and validation.

Why not pick a new area of interest every five years and do the same, albeit informally? First, study the brightest minds in the field. Next, stretch your mind to develop and test a new hypothesis, model or insight. Finally, after creating new knowledge or practices, ask others who are knowledgeable and supportive to review and refine your insights.

LEARN HOW TO LEARN

One of the great things about the world today is how accessible knowledge has become. Easy access to information has leveled the playing field, making it a lot easier for anyone to learn about any subject. Online courses, many for free, are affecting almost every field of study. For example, see Coursera (www.coursera.org), a site that offers free online courses from top learning institutions. Online communities of learners can communicate with like-minded individuals around the world. In the old days, we said, "Those who don't read are no better off than those who cannot read." Today, we say those who do not take advantage of all the learning resources available online are no better off than those who do not know how to access these resources.

Your next learning project may be to "learn how to learn" in today's world. If online learning is not your forte, think about connecting with someone who is adept at this skill. Find a way to let that person mentor you. If you have been in an organization for a time, a younger new-hire may bring this knowledge with him. You could offer to mentor him about the more traditional aspects of your organization, and let him mentor you on the finer points of learning in an interconnected world.

You are already learning about some of the twenty-five personal skills by reading this book. You can also delve deeper into any of the skills by going to www.TheCompleteLeader.org and selecting your area of interest. The companion website is one small example of the learning power of the Internet.

ASSESS THE LEVEL OF YOUR LEARNING

Dee Hock, founder of Visa and author of *One from Many: VISA and the Rise of Chaordic Organization*, defines different levels of learning as follows (emphasis added):

> Noise becomes <u>data</u> when it has a cognitive pattern. <u>Data</u> becomes <u>information</u> when assembled into a coherent whole, which can be related to other information. <u>Information</u> becomes <u>knowledge</u> when integrated with other information in a form useful for making decisions and determining actions. <u>Knowledge</u> becomes <u>understanding</u> when related to other knowledge in a manner useful in anticipating, judging and acting. <u>Understanding</u> becomes <u>wisdom</u> when informed by purpose, ethics, principles, memory and projection.

To be useful, your learning needs to at least be at the "knowledge" level—useful for making decisions and determining actions. As you continue your leadership journey, knowledge by itself will not make you successful. You will need understanding to inform more complex types of decisions and conceptual thinking. Knowledge and understanding will help you toward the final learning level, wisdom. In this way, you can fulfill your work and life in a way that serves both you and the greater good, and your journey will be intrinsically satisfying.

PROMOTE LEARNING IN YOUR ORGANIZATION

Become a champion for continuous learning in your organization. If there are already learning initiatives where you work, support them. You can also start your own learning initiatives: Begin informal lunches to promote continuous learning. Invite your staff members or other interested people. You might choose a book to discuss, or people could share what they learned at a conference or in a class. There are many ways to promote continuous learning. By surrounding yourself with others who are interested in learning, you will also be inspired to learn.

APPLY WHAT YOU LEARN

At the beginning of this module, we said continuous learning was about both learning and *applying* new concepts and methods. Once your learning becomes knowledge, you can put it into practice. You have not truly learned something until you have done it. A friend of ours had a math teacher who was fond of saying, "We learn to do by doing." First she explained the math concept, then she had her students apply the learning to solve several homework problems.

We have mentioned that much of an adult's learning comes from experience. Try out what you have been learning in your own "laboratory." Keep a journal of decisions you make and revisit them later to see how they stood the test of time. Observe the results and make corrections as needed. If something does not turn out as you anticipated, it is only a failure if you do not learn from the result; you will be condemned to repeat the mistake.

1.6

PROBLEM-SOLVING

WHAT IS PROBLEM-SOLVING?

MacGyver, a TV character on ABC in the mid-1980s and early 1990s, was the quintessential problem solver. A secret agent who did not carry a gun, he solved any complex problem using everyday materials that were lying around, along with his Swiss Army knife and duct tape. The show was so popular that to "MacGyver" something came to mean to creatively solve a problem.

> "You don't drown by falling in the water;
> you drown by staying there."
> – Edwin Louis Cole

People who are adept at problem-solving can anticipate, analyze, diagnose and deal with problems in an innovative way. Problem-solving ability also uses other skills discussed throughout Part One, including conceptual thinking, planning and organization, and creativity. Those who are less adept at dealing with problems and roadblocks will do some or all of the following: not see the problem coming; not be clear about who needs to be involved in solving it; misdiagnose or choose to solve the wrong problem; be unclear about where the problem begins and ends; be unwilling to change strategies; or decide on an approach too soon or too late. If you are not skilled at problem-solving, don't worry—like all twenty-five leadership competencies, there are ways to improve your capabilities as a leader.

WHY IS PROBLEM-SOLVING IMPORTANT?

Leaders get things done by working with and through others. Problems and roadblocks inevitably crop up along the way, and leaders with a well-honed ability to deal with problems are more effective at reaching their desired results. In fact, leaders who are problem solvers, and who mentor others who want to learn that skill, will always have an abundance of opportunity!

One challenge for leaders is determining what kind of problem they are dealing with. All problems cannot be dealt with in the same manner, and different kinds of problems require different approaches. Great leaders are able to adapt their strategies to fit specific challenges.

Let us consider two fundamentally different types of problems. The first type is a linear, or convergent—a "tame" problem. You can recognize this type of problem easily. It has well-known assumptions, finite and well-defined boundaries, accepted processes for achieving a solution, and one "right" or optimum answer. People involved in solving this type of problem will agree easily and quickly about what the problem is and what constitutes a valid solution. For example, a normal math problem or a broken machine on an assembly line are simple convergent problems.

The second type of problem is nonlinear, divergent and sometimes referred to as "wicked" or a "wicked mess." Wicked in this context does not mean evil. It means that the problem is "wicked hard" to solve, much like a "wicked" ski run is difficult to transverse without falling. Russell Ackoff, an American organizational theorist and consultant, wrote about these types of problems: "We have also come to realize that no problem ever exists in isolation. Every problem interacts with other problems and is therefore part of a set of interrelated problems, a system of problems. ... I choose to call such a system a mess."

> "Every adversity, every failure, every heartache carries with it the seed of an equal or greater benefit."
> – Napoleon Hill

These messy problems are not well-defined and have many unknowns. Boundary conditions are porous; that is, one problem interacts with and is affected by other problems. The contributing causes to the problem are not always clear and may change over time. Wicked messes have cultural, political, economic and value-based constraints, causing people to disagree about the nature, causes and solutions for this type of problem. The problem's definition and solution will change as the problem begins to be solved. Such problems do not have one right answer because the "right answer" varies depending on who you talk to. For example, as we write this book, there is a debate in the U.S. about guns and school safety. Some people say the solution to violence in schools is to tightly regulate who can legally obtain a gun and what types of firearms are legal. Another camp says the solution is to put armed security personnel in schools, along with other security measures. This complex issue has no simple, obvious answer everyone can easily agree on.

Convergent problems can be solved. Divergent problems are more "lived with" than solved. Examples of wicked messes include many social and/or strategic issues with long-time horizons, such as global climate change, homelessness, stopping the killing of innocent people, or nuclear waste disposal, to name a few.

All leaders are partially defined by the quality of their problem-solving and decision-making. Tomorrow's leaders will be faced with a turbulent, ambiguous and interconnected environment that involves even more wicked messes. Solving these complex issues will require greater dependency on clear communications among those involved, along with the use of computer-aided modeling software to allow various proposed solutions to be tried in compressed time. The leaders of tomorrow will no longer see themselves as master problem solvers, assuming responsibility as the expert in every situation. Instead, they will learn to be collaborative problem-solving *facilitators*. One of our friends describes this as "systemic problem management." The leader may not be the subject matter expert but understands and facilitates working on the problem, leading to collaborative results.

The world is already complex. As it becomes more so, the proportion of problems that are wicked messes will increase. Tame problems will be dealt with by people skilled in the particular field that is involved. Wicked messes will be grappled with by leaders. The ability to deal with wicked messes may become the hallmark of a great leader.

HOW IS PROBLEM-SOLVING LEARNED?

WHY BEFORE HOW

Before actually dealing with any problem, be sure to ask, "Why are we solving this problem?" You may be spending time trying to solve the wrong problem. Establish the "why" before spending any time and energy on the "how." Ask questions that point you to the "why," such as: Would a solution to this problem help us achieve our mission? Is this problem the root cause, or is it a symptom of a deeper cause?

Use the well-known "five whys" process, popularized by Toyota. To get beyond the perceived problem, ask "why" five times, or until you get to the root issue. It works like this:

> Boss, we've got a problem on the assembly line. The sawdust pump isn't working.

> Why? What is wrong? (Why #1)

> It lost its oil. It's dry and stuck.

> Why did that happen? (#2)

> The oil leaked out of the main seal. I think the seal is broken.

> Why do you think the seal may be broken? Didn't we replace the seal at the right time? (#3)

> Yes, we replaced the seal, but this latest one is from a new supplier.

> Why did we change suppliers? (#4)

> We were getting pressed by Finance to cut costs, and this supplier was less expensive.

We will stop the dialogue here because you can see how the problem shifts as you continue to delve into it by asking "why." This process also helps identify the type of problem you are facing. Convergent problems will yield to this type of diagnosis, while divergent problems tend to take different paths toward different but interconnected "root causes," depending on whom you talk to. For example, ask four people why there are homeless people on their streets, and you will get four different answers based on four different perceptions of the root cause.

> **"Erroneous assumptions can be disastrous."**
> **– Peter Drucker**

Before you start solving a perceived problem, make sure you are attacking the right problem and that you have determined whether this is a convergent, divergent, or "something in between" type of problem.

ANTICIPATE THE PROBLEM

The best approach to a problem is to anticipate it, and head it off before it occurs. Essentially, this is problem prevention. This is like using preemergent weed killer in the fall to prevent next spring's problems. Modules "1.2 Conceptual Thinking" and "1.3 Planning and Organization," will help with this part of problem-solving because they involve problem avoidance.

ANALYZE THE PROBLEM

When a problem does occur, cast a wide net to analyze what is going on. Talk with as many people as you can who are affected by the issue to help determine the boundaries of the problem. Ask the following kinds of questions:

How serious is it?

How widespread is it?

How long do we think it will last?

What will happen if we don't solve this?

Who owns this problem?

What would constitute an acceptable solution?

What data do we have to support what is going on?

Do not confuse assumptions with facts. Facts exist in an obvious, shared reality; for example, we can see that the machine is not working. Assumptions exist in one or more peoples' minds; for example, "I'll bet the framistat belt is broken again." Do not support assumptions over data. As the leader, you may have to make sure that data is respected and listened to, no matter who presents it. Too often, the person who delivers the message is seen as more important than what is said.

DIAGNOSE THE PROBLEM

If you are dealing with a definable problem, you can use the Plan-Do-Check-Act (PDCA) cycle discussed in "1.3 Planning and Organization," in combination with the "five whys" approach, to help with diagnosis. Diagnosis is the "check" part of that cycle.

In other words, the cycle goes like this: We had a Plan. We tried to implement (Do) the plan. Now, let us look at the results (Check) to figure out what to do next (Act). Many organizations have a defined problem-solving process, usually with six to eight steps; most of these are expansions of the PDCA cycle. You can find examples easily by searching "problem-solving process" on the web, or on *The Complete Leader* companion website at www.TheCompleteLeader.org.

CREATE A LIST OF STAKEHOLDERS' INTERESTS AND ALTERNATIVE SOLUTIONS

As people begin to recognize a problem, they typically think of a solution that suits their individual perspective on the issue. But that solution may not work for all involved, so it is important to first understand what matters to all stakeholders. During the analysis stage, check with all stakeholders to collect a list of things they care about. This "interests list" will become the common ground that will form the foundation of the problem-solving process. By measuring solutions against this list, you will be able to determine how comprehensive a particular solution will be. Remember: if major differences of opinion occur about the basic definition and boundary conditions of the problem, you are probably not dealing with a simple convergent problem. If so, review the earlier section again about how to respond to nonlinear, "wicked mess" problems.

As you clarify the gap between the situation and goal, people will suggest various solutions. Check to see how the solutions both close the gap and meet the desires of the interests list. You are now in the "how" part of the process, and in the "Plan" part of PDCA. Timing is important at this stage, so do not decide on one solution too soon or too late. If you do not take some time to look for alternative options, you may miss the best solution (see "1.4 Creativity" for ideas on how to generate alternatives). If you wait too long to make a decision, you may miss a window of opportunity or even create another problem.

> "Some problems are so complex that you have to be highly intelligent and well-informed just to be undecided about them."
>
> – Laurence J. Peter

SELECT AND IMPLEMENT A SOLUTION

Select a solution that appears to best solve the problem (see "1.7 Decision-Making" for more on this part of the process). Implement the chosen solution (the "Do" part of PDCA). Try the solution on a small scale if possible, and view this trial as an experiment to see what happens and what you can learn. Look for unintended consequences. Continue to make any adjustments as needed. Observe the solution working in place for some time (the "Check" part of PDCA), and make sure it does not have unintended side effects for any of the involved parties. Once you have done this, you will know the solution is really working, and full implementation can be completed.

WORKING WITH WICKED MESSES

As we have discussed, wicked messes do not have simple yes or no solutions. They have "better" or "worse" outcomes. These outcomes vary by perspective, and these types of problems are rarely solved, in the traditional sense. Because wicked messes are so complex and uncertain—with obscure and interrelated causes and, often, long time frames between cause and effect—leaders may tend to shy away from them. Nevertheless, these types of problems will become more common in the future, and tomorrow's leaders will not be able to ignore them.

Wicked messes are difficult to prepare for because each one is unique. The following approaches may make the mess easier to deal with:

Understand the mess. The mess, by definition, is broad in scope: it involves different systems interacting with each other. No one expert is likely to solve the mess, so the best chance of a positive outcome comes from having a deep understanding of all the systems involved and how they interact (for more on understanding systems, visit www.TheCompleteLeader.org). Take the time to create a safe space for dialogue where everyone involved can talk about their various values, issues and interests. You cannot work with a mess without first having a deep understanding of it.

Sort the problem. Upon examination of the wicked-complex problem, you may be able to find some sub-problems that can be solved and set aside, making the major issue more obvious. It is a bit like unraveling a tangled knot or necklace—as you untangle the first knot, the overall problem becomes simpler. Even after you do this, you may still have what looks like unresolvable issues. Be persistent, and keep sorting.

Suspend self-interest. Okay, maybe asking any person to suspend self-interest is unrealistic or too optimistic. But leaders must understand the need to transcend self-interest for the benefit of the greater whole. The point is: if people hunker down into positions (e.g. "I want this" and "I am not giving up that"), then there will be little chance of finding a workable path to a better solution. As the leader, keep the focus on shared interest.

Too often, groups only focus on their differences. Instead, create a list of all the things those involved care about, identify the group's common interests, and start from that point to look for solutions. This helps you work toward something they care about, rather than working against what they do not want.

For instance, using the previous example about safety in schools, the national conversation about gun control is in full sway in America as of this writing. As a nation, the shared interest we have in a solution is, obviously, a safer country by having fewer gun-related deaths. Most people also want children to have a safe place to learn, and for families to not be subjected to the trauma of having a loved one killed. Most of the population also cares about freedom and democracy in America. All of these items would go on the shared interest list. Any changes to the status quo, however, may impinge on one or more constituency's divergent interests—so the devil is in the details.

Be comfortable with ambiguity, paradoxes and dilemmas. During a decision-making process, patience is a virtue. Suspend your need to find a quick answer and, instead, sit with what appears to be a dilemma without a solution; sometimes, a way out of the mess will show up once you have a deeper understanding of the situation. Be patient. If you go for what appears to be a quick fix, it will likely lead to a longer-term problem—a so-called "fix that fails." Remember that the easy way out leads back in. As noted quality expert Dr. W. Edwards Deming once said, "Some things are unknown and unknowable."

Construct various scenarios or models of different futures.
People working on a mess can create several different stories about the future to help them envision the implications of decisions. These might include a preferred future, a doomsday future, a probable future and a utopian future (see our discussion of scenario planning in "1.1 Futuristic Thinking"). When constructing these futures, especially look for previously unexpected characteristics or results that may emerge and affect the mess in the future. This type of modeling can also draw out assumptions and values participants may not have stated, which will help to deepen the shared understanding of the problem.

DECISION-MAKING

WHAT IS DECISION-MAKING?

On January 15, 2009, US Airways flight 1549 was on a routine flight from LaGuardia airport in New York to Charlotte, NC. Shortly after takeoff, the plane flew through a flock of Canadian geese. Both engines lost thrust. The captain had about thirty seconds to decide how to save his own life and the lives of the 154 people on board. While talking with the control tower, he considered, and rejected, the options of going back to LaGuardia and diverting to Teterboro in New Jersey. Instead, he decided to put the 76-ton airliner into the Hudson River. Captain Chesley "Sully" Sullenberger's quick thinking and decisive action saved all 154 people. The "Miracle on the Hudson" is now part of airplane lore, and an inspiring example of decision-making under pressure.

Decision-making is the process of resolving and responding to problems in the best possible way by making an informed choice from a number of options. People who have a well-developed decision-making competency can make difficult decisions in a timely manner, even under intense pressure, as Captain Sullenberger did. They gather relevant facts, data and opinions and develop a rationale to make the decision. They consider the impact of the decision on everyone involved and own the decision they make.

People who have not yet developed a competency for decision-making tend to make decisions they should not and delay making decisions they should. Decisions tend to be based more on "gut feel" or emotion and less on a clear awareness of details and facts. They may not consider all of the side effects of their decisions, including the impact on others.

> **"In God we trust, all others bring data."**
> **– Dr. W. Edwards Deming**

Decision-making is a mental process that results in a choice. The choice, picked from one or more alternatives, leads to an action. So, decisions create actions. Recent discoveries in neuropsychology indicate that there are two distinct aspects in the mental process of decision-making. Scientists think that up to 90 percent of our decisions are made subconsciously, with our subconscious mind selling its accumulated biases to our conscious mind. Of course, most of the time, we think we are making a totally conscious decision. This discovery begs the question, "How does our subconscious mind develop its biases?" The answer lies in some combination of genetics and experience. The good news is that, regardless of our genetic makeup at conception, we can enhance our decision-making acumen through continuous learning and beneficial experiences.

A person who makes a decision uses some of the other skills listed in "Part One: Leaders Are Clear Thinkers," such as conceptual thinking, planning and organization, and problem-solving. All of these thinking skills are interrelated. In this module, we will concentrate on the processes and rules that underpin a leader's ability to make the right decision at the right time.

WHY IS DECISION-MAKING IMPORTANT?

Decisions drive behaviors. Behaviors create life. Someone once said that if you want to understand your present circumstances, look at your past behaviors; if you want to understand your future, look at your present behaviors.

We all make innumerable decisions daily, most of which are made automatically. They seem obvious to us. Our decisions range from simple (chocolate or strawberries for dessert) to complex (whether a company invests in a new facility). Timelines and consequences of our decisions run from the immediate to far in the future.

Leadership is about taking an idea and making it happen through the efforts of the people involved. Every project can be defined by the decisions made to create it. As a leader, you must make wise, effective, timely decisions. Leaders who do more things right (and fewer things wrong) are the ones who make the best decisions, while considering the needs and interests of the group.

As we have pointed out in other modules, the future continues to get more complex and more uncertain with shorter and shorter lead times to get things done. This will put even more pressure on leaders to quickly make effective decisions in an increasingly ambiguous environment.

HOW IS DECISION-MAKING LEARNED?

An old line goes, "Experience is what you get when you don't get what you want." Experience is helpful for decisions where the results are seen shortly after the decision is made. For other decisions, humans do not live long enough to learn from experience. In *Management Challenges for the 21st Century*, Peter Drucker wrote, "Whenever you make a key decision or take a key action, write down what you expect will happen. Nine or twelve months later, compare the actual results with your expectations. I have been practicing this method for fifteen to twenty years now, and every time I do it, I am surprised."

You can also intentionally follow some other behaviors to help you make important decisions. Here are some tips to help you eliminate some of the more obvious errors during decision-making:

EXAMINE THE DECISION

First, be clear with yourself about the decision itself. Ask yourself and others, "Is this the right decision for us to be making at this time?" This is similar to the "Why Before How" discussion in "1.6 Problem-Solving." For instance, should we be deciding on manpower numbers for next year right now, or are there other decisions that need to be made first? What will happen if we do not make this decision now?

Another aspect of examining the decision is to ask, "Whose decision is this?" Be clear about what decisions you must make because of the position you occupy. There are a small number of decisions that, because of rules, procedures or laws, belong to a certain position. For instance, suppose that Josie is the CFO of a small company with a policy that any expense over $10,000 must be approved by the CFO. That decision cannot be delegated to someone else. Similarly, there are numerous decisions on other matters that Josie might be able to delegate. If she chooses to make decisions that are better suited for others, she may be accused, rightly, of micromanaging and taking away decisions that can and should be made by those on her team.

Ron recommends that his clients place their decisions into one of four categories, based on how much control the decision-maker needs to keep:

- A **dictatorial decision** is made by the decision-maker at least 90 percent of the time. There is no discussion, just implementation. This type of decision may be used during times of crises.

- An **authoritative decision** is still made by the decision-maker, often after talking with others. An example of an authoritative decision is a long-term strategic decision.

- A **consultative decision** takes place when the decision-maker gives the problem to the people involved. They make recommendations for solutions, and the decision-maker has the final say.

- A **participative decision** occurs when the decision-maker lets those involved make the choice, after giving them any boundaries or guidelines that could affect their decision. This type of decision-making can be used to develop cultural norms.

An effective leader is not only a great decision-maker but also recognizes when a choice should be delegated. Always ask yourself, "Is this the right decision to make now?" and "Is this my decision to make?"

COLLECT ALL POSSIBLE DATA

As we have mentioned throughout "Part One: Leaders Are Clear Thinkers," collecting and accepting all pertinent data is necessary to sound decision-making. The data helps you form a rationale for the decision. Do not fall prey to the "not invented here" syndrome, which screens out information that comes from a different source or does not align with your initial thoughts. Instead, accept it with appreciation. New ideas come from differences of opinion, different sources and different views. If you only ask for feedback or information from people who see the problem as you see it, known as "groupthink," you will likely miss something. Ask yourself, "Who else might have some ideas about this problem?" and "Has a similar problem been solved in some other place?" With both, the trick is to learn from other examples but not be limited by them.

MAKE TIMELY DECISIONS

Randy has a habit of delaying decision-making, in the guise of getting more data. One day, his manager said to him, "Randy, I am paying you to make decisions. If you wait until all the facts are in, it is not a decision. It is a fact." On the other hand, Ron has been guilty of making decisions based on opinions instead of data. Effective leaders make timely decisions. They find a balance between accepting the first option that seems like it might work and not making the decision until it makes itself. Ask yourself, "When is the optimal time to make this decision?" and "When will it be too late to make this decision?"

UNDERSTAND THAT EVERY DECISION IS A HUMAN DECISION

Few, if any, decisions made by leaders do not impact people. Effective decision-making includes considering its effect on all affected parties. Make it your practice to consider multiple bottom lines for every decision, including at least financial, personal and ecological impacts.

> "The key to my success has been that I was right in my decisions...51 percent of the time."
> – Jim Zamzow, entrepreneur and innovator

Ask yourself, "Who needs to support this decision and help implement it?" "Who will need to change what they do because of this decision?" and "Will anyone be adversely affected by this decision? If so, how can we minimize the negative impact?"

OWN YOUR DECISIONS

An effective leader accepts the consequences of the decisions she makes. An ineffective leader blames bad decisions on external forces—someone or something else. Not all of your decisions will be right the first time, but remember that a baseball hitter who gets on base a third of the time is an asset to the team. A surgeon who only completes a third of his operations successfully will not be a surgeon for long. What is acceptable in your field?

As the workplace becomes more interconnected and ambiguous, the chances of making a correct decision go down. We mentioned in "1.6 Problem-Solving" that the concept of "one right answer" does not make sense for some highly-complex problems known as "wicked messes." Unintended consequences and changing boundary conditions play havoc with normal decision-making. That is the world we live in. Embrace that, do your homework and do not be afraid to act.

> "When you want it bad, you get it bad."
> – Unknown

The effective leader not only owns her decision but also, when results vary from expectations, learns from her mistakes and makes corrections. There are two points here: 1) Own your decisions, and 2) Be willing to change them when appropriate. Less effective leaders let their egos impact their decision-making and are unwilling to either admit a mistake or make a timely change.

GET A PROCESS

Decisions vary from the simple ones to the wicked messes. For decisions that are not too messy, having a specific process that you can use and share with others is helpful. Many books and websites explain six-to-eight-step processes, which usually cover both problem-solving and decision-making.

For instance, Xerox has advocated the following six-step problem-solving process for its dealers. The actual decision-making part of the process occurs at step four.

1. Identify and select the problem.

2. Analyze the problem.

3. Generate potential solutions.

4. Select and plan a specific solution.

5. Implement that solution.

6. Evaluate the solution.

We do not discount using intuition and "gut feel" to make decisions, when appropriate. However, these intuitive or right-brain approaches can be even more effective when partnered with well-developed rationale based on a process. Use your whole brain, and the brains of others, to solve problems.

PART 2:

LEADERS LEAD THEMSELVES

Leading others first involves being able to lead yourself. If you have some skill at leading yourself, which means you are productive, you will eventually be recognized as someone who can get things done. "Leading by example" is the idea behind leading yourself.

In Part Two, we will focus on five personal competencies that help leaders lead themselves. There are innumerable ways people stumble in their careers and lose their right to lead; the competencies will help minimize those risks.

These competencies are more than just tools. They overlap and work together synergistically to help you focus—to keep the main thing the main thing. We discuss them in the order they usually happen in any given project or situation:

2.1 Self-Management – Ability to prioritize goals and decide what you need to do, and ability to manage self in terms of physical, mental, social and spiritual realms

2.2 Personal Accountability – Ability to take personal responsibility for processes, decisions, actions and results created by you

2.3 Flexibility – Ability to change plans to match reality

2.4 Resiliency – Ability to persevere and keep going when difficulties arise

2.5 Goal Achievement – Ability to execute, to get desired results

To use a sports analogy, self-management means getting yourself in shape to play, physically and mentally, and being willing to practice and "pay the price" for a future victory. Personal account-ability helps your teammates count on you, because they know you are responsible for doing your part for the team without making excuses. Flexibility and resiliency are necessary during the game. Those skills help you respond in the moment to what is actually happening on the field, without being a slave to the pre-game plan or getting down when the other team scores. Goal achievement is the ability to score the winning point when the chips are down—to perform at a high level when it counts and "refuse to lose."

It is easy to recognize a person who is skilled in the five self-leader-ship competencies: she exhibits particular behaviors, such as clari-fying and communicating what is important and managing time and priorities. Someone who is not as skilled in these competencies exhibits different behaviors, including not admitting mistakes, blaming others, being too risk averse and wasting precious time.

Remember, behaviors are driven by what people value as impor-tant—what motivates them. Take a minute to think about a suc-cessful independent business person or entrepreneur you know, such as a farmer, a self-employed accountant or a dentist. Every day, for many years, he does whatever needs to be done to be successful. Why?

We mentioned that Randy's dad was an architect and home builder. He had several skilled carpenters who worked with him, but he was responsible for all facets of his business. If he had not met with the clients, gotten the necessary permits, drawn the plans, ordered the supplies, organized the work, sent out the invoices, paid the bills, and done all the other innumerable things it takes to run a small business, he would not have had a business.

Randy's dad loved his family and his community, he enjoyed helping people, and he had a talent for designing and building homes. His business was a way for him to use his talent to do the things he loved. His self-managing behaviors resulted from his intrinsic motivators. If success is measured by how many friends a person has, he was immensely successful.

DISCOVER YOUR INTRINSIC MOTIVATION

Self-managed people are typically working because they "want to," not because they "have to." Making the connection between what you want, or "why" you do what you do, is foundational to leadership, as well as to success in any endeavor. For example, researchers and engineers are often motivated by solving problems and figuring things out. Salespeople may be motivated by getting a return on their personal investment of time, talent and effort. Artists, designers and craftsmen are motivated by creating something unique and beautiful. Teachers and nurses are motivated by helping those who need help. Many leaders are motivated by being in charge—being a leader. Still others, such as ministers and police, are motivated by adhering to a set of rules that describe right and wrong.

Most of us are motivated by more than one thing. If you can identify your core motivators and link them to what you are doing, both in your career and on a daily basis, you will be more willing to do what you need to do now, to get what you want in the future. Keep this idea of intrinsic motivation in mind as you explore this part of the book.

In "1.6 Problem-Solving," under "Why Before How," we explained the "five whys." You can also use the "whys" to zero in on your intrinsic motivators. For example:

Q: What is important to you?

A: Making money.

Q: Why is making money important to you?

A: Because one of my most important roles is to provide for my family.

Q: Why is taking care of your family important to you?

A: Because they are the most important things in my life.

Maybe it only takes you two or three "whys" instead of five to get to a deeper emotionally or spiritually based answer. This deeper answer is the root cause that taps into an important intrinsic motivator—and probably one of your basic values. For more ideas on identifying your intrinsic motivators, see also "Choose Who You Want to Be" in "1.0 Getting Started" and "Identify Your Passions" in "1.5 Continuous Learning."

Now, let us take a look at each of these important personal competencies in more detail.

SELF-MANAGEMENT

WHAT IS SELF-MANAGEMENT?

Dear Ron,

> I've been out of college five years and had eight jobs. None of them lasted over nine months. The people I worked with were not nice to me, and the jobs were not very good either. I am not sure I am cut out for the work world. I feel like I wasted my time getting my degree. Can you help me find a decent job?
>
> Signed,
> Grumpy

Dear Grumpy,

> What do you see as the common element in all the jobs you have had and all the people you worked with? That is right—you! If you want to be happy in your work, you need to realize that it is your job, not anybody else's, to make that happen. Your first management job is with yourself. If you want to be happy and become someone people want to work with, then be upbeat and interested in those around you. Be helpful. Do

your job and a little more. Do for them what you would like them to do for you. Make an effort to be someone others want to work with. You may find they will be more interested in you, and that your jobs will begin to get better.

Signed,
Ron

Self-management means demonstrating self-control and managing time and priorities appropriately. A person skilled in self-management can work independently, without direct supervision, to pursue business objectives. He is able to prioritize the activities that are most important to complete a task and minimize distractions and time-wasters to complete high-quality work within a specified time frame.

> "Tell me how a young man spends his evenings and I will tell you how far he is likely to go in the world ...
> If he diligently utilizes his own time ... to fit himself for more responsible duties, then the greater responsibilities—and greater rewards—are almost certain to come to him."
> – B. C. Forbes, Scottish author and financial journalist who founded *Forbes Magazine*

A person lacking self-management skills tends to become distracted by unimportant things. He does not have a clear sense of priorities or grasp of what needs to be done to complete a task. He may not be in the physical or mental state needed to do excellent work and will require more direct supervision than others.

WHY IS SELF-MANAGEMENT IMPORTANT?

Imagine a leader who cannot take care of himself, who lacks self-control, who is unclear about what needs to be done next, or who cannot be trusted. Would you follow him? After all, even people who are *not* contemplating becoming leaders must exhibit self-management skills for most jobs. People who can see what needs to be done and can manage themselves are always appreciated.

So, certainly, people who want to be leaders must first demonstrate that they can lead themselves.

Self-management is not a new skill. Every period in history had its share of leaders who got off track because they did not manage themselves appropriately. This will probably not change, but seeing poor examples of self-management helps demonstrate why this skill is so important.

In the future, the need for self-management will be magnified. More work will be done remotely, often contributing to results that will be realized somewhere else in the world. Greater so-called "spans of control" will mean that many people will have less direct management than they have had in the past. Team members will be assigned larger chunks of work without a specific blueprint for how to accomplish it. This remote work environment, coupled with an ever-increasing desire to get things done quicker, means that getting the results leaders want requires that everyone involved is clear about their roles and willing to work without someone checking their every move.

Tomorrow's leaders will also face a transparent communication medium, making virtually everything public knowledge. Issues of competence or character will not go unnoticed, and failing to be a self-manager will carry negative consequences for their careers.

> **"Position does not make the man or a great leader, it's how you use it."**
> **- David Butler**

HOW IS SELF-MANAGEMENT LEARNED?

DEVELOP SELF-CONTROL

Self-control is the ability to control your desires, emotions and behaviors, rather than have them control you. This is a key part of emotional intelligence and self-management. One way to develop more self-control is to take care of yourself physically. When you are well-rested, not overloaded with stress, eating a healthy diet and getting exercise, you will find it easier to control your emotions and mental clarity. Having a larger reason to control yourself—an intrinsic motivator—can also make self-management easier to practice (see introduction to Part Two for more on motivators). Self-control may even come quite naturally to you.

In his timeless book, *The 7 Habits of Highly Effective People*, Dr. Stephen R. Covey makes the distinction between proactive and reactive behavior. Proactive behavior involves choosing your own response to a stimulus, or a particular situation. Reactive behavior means blaming the stimulus for your behavior. "She made me mad" or "I had no choice" are examples of reactive language. When you think and act in a reactive way, you give up your ability to choose your response—you make yourself a victim. Proactive behavior is self-control. Reactive behavior is allowing a thing, person or event to dictate your behavior. Ask yourself, "What can I choose to do that is within my control, to move my work forward?"

> "There are many options; there is only one next step."
> – David Allen

CLARIFY WHAT IS IMPORTANT

Self-management involves clarifying what is important in your work. There is an old saying, "If you don't know where you are going, any road will do." Make sure that you know the expectations about your work. These include such things as desired results, timelines, ways of measuring success, available resources, interdependencies, and guidelines for staying in communication and out of trouble. Be explicit, and do not assume that others see a project as you do. Be sure you are clear about expectations at the start. Nothing is more frustrating than doing a lot of "good" work, only to find out that it was not needed. Ask yourself, "Have I created an agreement with the people I work with, detailing who is doing what, by when?"

> **"The enemy of the 'best' is often the 'good.'"**
> **– Dr. Stephen R. Covey**

MANAGE TIME AND PRIORITIES

Once you clarify what is important and establish project timelines for completion, then you can put together individual timelines and internal checkpoints to make sure you do not fall behind schedule. All leaders have some type of scheduling and prioritizing process, and there are many types of gadgets and software available to help you "keep the main thing the main thing." The most important criteria for any system is that it must be one you will use consistently and exclusively. If you use a task application on your smartphone or computer, for example, you must resist the temptation to keep creating to-do lists on multiple slips of paper.

Knowing what priorities need to be completed, by when, allows you to mentally construct a timeline—in essence, creating the project in your mind. Make sure to break any large task into doable bite-size chunks with their own completion milestones. Once you know what you need to accomplish on a daily and weekly basis, a large project will not look so formidable, and it will be easier to stay on schedule (see "Select Appropriate Tools" in "1.3 Planning and Organization" for more on managing time and priorities). Ask yourself, "What is the highest and best use of my time this week?" Or, use the advice of David Allen, author of *Getting Things Done*, and ask yourself, "What is the next action I need to take?" This question will keep you focused on your priorities and moving forward.

MINIMIZE DISRUPTIONS

All of us fall prey to disruptions and time-wasters. When this happens, it is a good opportunity to learn from experience. Notice what is taking you away from your main work. One way to do this is to schedule a week in advance and put the priorities on your calendar. Again, to quote Dr. Stephen R. Covey, "Put first things first." Then, keep track on your calendar of how you spend your time, compared to how you planned to spend it. Then, check back at the end of the week and compare the two.

> **"If you want to have more, you have to become more."**
>
> **– Jim Rohn**

What got done and what did not? Be honest with yourself. Of course, there will be some unplanned interruptions during the week. There will be other distractions that got in the way of your productivity—and some are not-so-important things. Come up with a countermeasure to block that time-waster, and implement your countermeasure the next week. Continue this weekly review until you are happy with your productivity. You cannot control everything, but by eliminating a few productivity-drainers, you can become much more productive. Eliminate as many distractions as you can that are not contributing to getting your real work done.

MAINTAIN ACTIVITY

"A grade-B plan with grade-A execution beats a grade-A plan with grade-B execution," as the adage goes. Behaviors create results. If you have adopted the ideas we have offered for improving self-management, then you will have dealt with many roadblocks. You still need to perform—to do the work needed to create value and get the result (see "2.5 Goal Achievement" for more tips on getting things done). Some people naturally move to action; others do not. Maintaining activity may be second nature to you. If it is not, keep in mind why you are doing the work and what needs to get done today to move things forward. The desire to achieve is fueled by a high internal standard for performance that you hold yourself to. Maintain your internal standards, and balance that by appreciating your accomplishments. Ask yourself, "What do I need to do (observable behaviors) this week? How will I measure success?"

> "Who you are speaks so loudly I can't hear what you say."
> – Ralph Waldo Emerson

PERSONAL ACCOUNTABILITY

WHAT IS PERSONAL ACCOUNTABILITY?

In the late 1890s, there was increasing tension between the United States and Spain, who then ruled Cuba. United States President William McKinley wanted to establish a relationship with the Cuban rebels—a relationship that could prove valuable if war broke out between the U.S. and Spain. McKinley asked for the name of a person who could take a letter to the rebels' leader, Colonel Garcia, and was given the name of American Captain Andrew Rowan.

No one knew where Garcia was—just that he was somewhere in the mountain jungles of Cuba. McKinley needed to get a message to him quickly. Rowan took the letter McKinley wrote, sealed it in an oil-skin pouch, and left for Cuba. Four days later, he arrived by boat and went into the jungle. He eventually found Garcia in the Oriente Mountains and established a rapport with him, gaining information from Garcia that helped the U.S. fight the Spanish. Three weeks later, Rowan came out the other side of the island, having delivered the letter to Garcia.

In March 1899, artist and publisher Elbert Hubbard wrote an untitled article about Rowan's mission for *The Philistine* magazine. He detailed that Rowan exhibited personal accountability (although he used different words) in carrying out his mission. To quote from the article:

> The point that I wish to make is this: McKinley gave Rowan a letter to be delivered to Garcia; Rowan took the letter and did not ask, "Where is he at?" ... It is not book-learning young men need, nor instruction about this and that, but a stiffening of the vertebrae which will cause them to be loyal to a trust, to act promptly, concentrate their energies: do the thing—"Carry a message to Garcia." ...
>
> And the man who, when given a letter for Garcia, quietly takes the missive, without asking any idiotic questions, and with no lurking intention of chucking it into the nearest sewer, or of doing aught else but deliver it, never gets "laid off," nor has to go on strike for higher wages. Civilization is one long anxious search for just such individuals. Anything such a man asks shall be granted. His kind is so rare that no employer can afford to let him go. He is wanted in every city, town and village—in every office, shop, store and factory.
>
> The world cries out for such: he is needed, and needed badly—the man who can carry a message to Garcia.

Hubbard's article might have been the first written piece to ever "go viral." It was reprinted as a pamphlet and later as a book with the title *A Message To Garcia*. Industrial and military leaders loved its message, and ordered copies for their employees and troops. More than 40 million copies were sold; it was so popular that it was translated into thirty-seven languages. Two movies were made about the journey. For years, "to take a message to Garcia" was slang for taking initiative.

Personal accountability is the willingness and ability to take personal responsibility for processes, decisions, actions and results created by you. People who have developed the competency of personal accountability do not need someone else to "hold them" accountable. Instead, they hold themselves accountable. They can be counted on. They *are* accountable for their actions and behaviors. They are responsible for returning calls on time, spending less than they earn, maintaining important relationships, and keeping physically and mentally fit. At work, they take responsibility for doing their job for the team. If they make a mistake, they admit it and learn from it. On a project, they understand what they need to do and work professionally and competently. As a result of their actions, they are trusted, respected and sought out to help on important projects.

The previous module on self-management was about the ability to prioritize personal goals and decide what you need to do; self-management and personal accountability reinforce one another. Someone who has good self-management skills will find it easier to be personally accountable, and someone who has developed personal accountability will find it easier to manage his or her emotions, behaviors and results. We like the definition provided by our friends, Steve and Jill Morris of Choiceworks: personal accountability is owning the consequences of your choices in delivering the agreed-to results and helping others do the same.

People who have not yet developed personal accountability wait to be told what to do and make a minimal effort to get the job done. They say things like "it's not my job" and "nobody told me." They also need more direct supervision and have more trouble getting their work completed on time with high quality. Such people easily get off-track and are pulled toward what is in front of them, rather than focusing on what needs to be done. The unaccountable often blame their poor choices on someone or something else. They may not be trusted and respected and may be considered lazy by people they work with. The good news is that, regardless of whether a person has been accountable in the past, anyone can choose to develop more personal accountability in the present and future.

WHY IS PERSONAL ACCOUNTABILITY IMPORTANT?

Of the twenty-five competencies in this book, personal accountability may be the skill needed in the highest percentage of jobs. What job does not need someone who will commit to the task at hand, without complaints or excuses? And this competency will not be any less important in the years to come. Because of the interdependence of tomorrow's work, and the geographically diverse population contributing to that work, being able to rely on people to complete their part of a project will be even more important. For people who want long-term success in leadership roles, demonstrating personal accountability is an absolute must.

As a leader, you may be a part of, and be responsible to, boards of directors. Leaders who demonstrate personal accountability with their boards are transparent, coachable and results-driven, even when things do not turn out as planned. They bring reasons for the results to the board, not excuses. What is the difference? Though the distinction may often be subtle, accountable leaders help others understand the context and constraints that have impacted the results without abdicating full responsibility for their role as leaders. One of the most powerful demonstrations of this type of personal accountability is when a leader presents the facts within context and then submits to the judgment of others regarding the extent of his accountability for the results.

> **"If it is to be, it is up to me."**
> **– Unknown**

Personally accountable board members are prepared, respectful and engaged. They look for ways to add value to the board. They know what is expected as responsible, proactive members. They know the difference between advising, meddling and abdicating, and they fulfill their roles as acts of service, not as a way to garner status. As such, highly developed personal accountability helps make you a great leader and board member.

HOW IS PERSONAL ACCOUNTABILITY LEARNED?

MAKE THE CHOICE

As with many of our competencies, the first step is to decide that you are accountable for your thoughts and behaviors. Once you claim this responsibility, it will be much easier to decide what to do in any situation. Just ask yourself, "What is the right thing for me to do now to be personally accountable?"

KNOW WHAT IS EXPECTED

It is impossible to be accountable for something until you are clear about what it is. The basic difference between accountability and blame is simple: accountability is chosen before the fact; blame is handed out afterward. Accountability is clarified and agreed to *before* you make any commitment.

An effective way to clarify expectations is to ask stakeholders, "What are the key results that will reflect superior performance in my job, to this project or for our team?" It is not unusual to find that different parties have different expectations. It is much better to discover these differences early so you can reach a consensus on expectations; otherwise, it may become too late to satisfy everyone's needs.

TAKE OWNERSHIP

Once you have clarified your personal commitment to completing a project, the next step is to take ownership of what needs to be done. In business, both "renters" and "owners" exist in the workplace. The renters are there to make a buck and then get on with their life. They do not feel a commitment to the whole organization or the overall success of the enterprise. They may be good people, and they may earn their fair day's pay, but they will not "do whatever is necessary" to make sure the company succeeds.

> **"It is up to me and no one else to make sure I am doing what I know I should be doing."**
> **– Todd Smith**

Recently, Randy's wife was standing in line at the post office at about 4:45 in the evening. She was third in line, waiting to put postage on a small package. Two clerks were working. One was doing his best to make putting postage on eight boxes last all day. The other clerk was finishing up with a customer. As soon as the second clerk completed the transaction, he put his "next window" sign up and left, grabbing his coat and heading out the back door, oblivious to the line of waiting customers. Perhaps he had a family emergency. However, he may also have been a "renter" who decided he was not getting paid to improve the quality of customer service within the organization. In fact, neither clerk seemed concerned about customer service.

LOOK FOR YOUR PART IN THE SITUATION

When something goes wrong, personally accountable people look at themselves first, self-evaluate and ask questions like, "What was my part in this situation?" or "What could I have done to achieve the goal?" Steve Morris told us the following story:

> Bob, a client, called me recently and told me that Jack, who reported to Bob, was failing in his job. I asked Bob what he had done to support Jack. There was dead silence for about thirty seconds, and then Bob replied, "I've done nothing to help him since he started here six months ago, when I shared

my expectations. I have not given him any feedback. He's a vice president, and I assumed he would know what to do. I need to clarify both my expectations and his, and give him some additional direction."

Accountable people are proactive about finding the root cause to a problem, even if the answer points to themselves.

ADMIT MISTAKES

Part of being personally accountable is the ability to admit a mistake when you make one. This is not easy to do. Ego, guilt, pride, and not wanting to appear weak or diminished all keep people from admitting mistakes. Why *should* you admit an error? Reason number one is because you have decided to be personally accountable. Paradoxically, leaders who appropriately apologize are often respected and seen in a more favorable light. None of us is perfect. Why pretend to be?

Ron worked with an executive who was misled by a subordinate; as a result, she prematurely challenged the integrity of a significant business partner overseas. When she realized her error, she flew to Japan to apologize face-to-face. She did not blame her subordinate but instead took full responsibility for her actions. Instead of a fractured and irreparable business relationship, she won the respect of her Japanese business partner because of her willingness to fully admit her mistake.

Admitting an error is a courageous act. People who choose to do this courageous act build their self-efficacy. They become internally stronger and grow from the experience. After you admit fault once, it becomes easier.

> "The buck stops here."
> – Harry Truman

Acknowledging responsibility also brings the incident to light and helps you make better choices in the future. Some people say a mistake is only a mistake if you do not learn from it. Errors are opportunities to learn. As a leader, you want to create a place where mistakes are dealt with and learned from, not covered up. When an error occurs, encourage your team to look to the process to see what led to the error. This approach is in contrast to organizations that focus on questions like, "Who goofed up?"

USE AFTER ACTION REVIEWS

After action reviews (AARs), a process that originated in the U.S. Army, go beyond admitting mistakes to also focus on successes that can be repeated. Many companies are adopting some form of AAR to analyze their projects and learn from them. If done correctly, an AAR can be a powerful source for organizational learning. The four basic questions used in the AAR are:

1. What did we intend to accomplish? (What was our strategy?)

2. What did we do? (What was the difference between strategy and execution?)

3. Why did it happen that way? (Why was there a difference between strategy and execution?)

4. What will we do to adapt our strategy or execution for better outcomes? (How do we repeat our success and not repeat our mistake?)

What separates AARs from more traditional "postmortems" is twofold. First, the AAR process typically spends 50 percent or more of the time focusing on the "why." This is where learning occurs. The purpose of AARs is learning, not blame. Second, AARs are a part of an organization's culture and occur after every significant success or failure. They are not an exception—and not a witch hunt.

If you decide to use AARs, do the process completely. As a leader, it will be your job to make sure AARs are completed after both successes and failures, and to make sure the findings get implemented into future actions. Otherwise, the AAR will become one more fad to be briefly sampled and then forgotten.

DO MORE THAN ASKED

When you are personally accountable, you treat your job like an owner. You also work like a "volunteer." You work because you want to, not only because you have to. People who volunteer choose to give their discretionary energy, over and above the minimum needed, and do whatever it takes to get the job done. They err on the side of doing more, not less. Look for opportunities to go beyond what is expected. Ask yourself, "What else needs to be done here?"

USE FEEDBACK ABOUT HOW YOU ARE PERCEIVED

Personal accountability means taking responsibility for your actions—including how your actions affect others. Make sure your impact is positive and in line with your intent. Do not assume that everyone is happy with your performance. Instead, solicit feedback from the people you interact with.

This process can be as easy as asking, "Are you getting what you need from me, and do you need everything you are getting?" Another tried and true method is to ask your customers what they want you to continue doing, start doing and stop doing. If you have recurring meetings, consider including a quick survey at the end of each meeting.

Another place to receive feedback is during the AAR process (see "Use After Action Reviews" earlier in this module). It is important that feedback flows freely in all directions. If you have a leadership role, encourage both your peers and subordinates to be honest with you about your performance. Thank people for both the positive and negative feedback you get.

Whit Mitchell, our associate and a successful executive coach, teaches his clients to ask for specific feedback on the behavior they want to improve. For instance, if Whit is helping a leader become more patient and listen more effectively, he might ask someone attending a meeting to mark on a sheet of paper how many times the leader interrupted others, and to give that information to the leader at the end of the meeting. Or, he may ask someone else to keep track of how much time the leader is listening and how much time she is talking. Whit even provides a stopwatch. He believes that the more specific and documentable the feedback, the more valuable it becomes.

It is important to thank people for feedback. It is even more important to show them you are listening and that you value their feedback by putting their suggestions into practice. Make changes where needed. This trait will show up again in our next competency, which is flexibility. Asking for and implementing feedback is another example of learning from experience.

In summary, as you work on becoming more personally accountable:

1. Be sure you clearly understand and can state what is expected of you.

2. Do what is expected, and more.

3. Seek feedback on how to improve, and respect that feedback by making changes that help you grow as a leader.

FLEXIBILITY

Think about a tall tree when the wind is blowing. The tree, which looks rigid on a calm day, moves and bends with the wind. It is flexible when under stress but not so flexible that it blows over. There is also a resilience about trees, and nature in general, that balances the bending with appropriate resistance and allows trees to adjust to change. Both flexibility and resilience are needed for long-term growth of a tree, a person or an organization, which is why those qualities are the next two competencies in "Part Two: Leaders Lead Themselves."

Ron learned another metaphor when he was working in Asia. An associate explained the significance of the ancient Chinese coin that is circular on the outside and has a square hole in the center. The circular shape symbolizes the flexibility and "softness" appropriate for interacting with others and responding to a constantly changing environment. The square hole in the center represents the resilience and "hardness" of core values, commitments and issues of character.

Flexibility is the ability to change plans in response to current realities. People who are flexible are able to recognize the dynamic circumstances and adapt tactics in order to achieve the desired result. They respond promptly to shifts in direction, accept new ideas and adapt their personal styles to work with different people. They maintain productivity during transitions or periods of chaos.

WHAT IS FLEXIBILITY?

Imagine that the clock is winding down in the fourth quarter of an American football game, and the home team is five points behind. It is third down with two yards to go to get a first down. Everyone in the stadium knows that the safe play is to run the ball and pick up the yardage to keep the drive alive.

The quarterback, Peyton, brings his team to the scrimmage line and looks at the defense. All of a sudden, he starts barking words like a man possessed: "Taco! Taco! 14 blue! 14 blue!" He dances around, pointing, making sure all his teammates hear this strange language. The play clock is at three seconds. His team makes a few slight shifts. With the clock at one second, the center snaps the ball. Peyton fakes to the fullback and lobs a pass. The tight end catches it—just over the outstretched arms of the blitzing defense—and scores!

Peyton Manning is known for being able to read a defense and adjust his offense on the fly. His flexibility gives his team an edge over other quarterbacks who are less adept or who get their plays from the sideline.

Flexibility is the ability to be agile in adapting to changes, to handle different situations in different ways. A person with a well-developed capacity for flexibility will respond promptly to shifts in direction, priorities and schedules. He embraces and champions change, is open to new ideas and methods, and can adapt his personal style to work with a wide spectrum of people. He is willing to modify his approach to respond to changing circumstances.

> "Every problem has in it the seeds of its own solution. If you don't have any problems, you don't get any seeds."
> – Dr. Norman Vincent Peale

A person who is not as adept at flexibility may perform acceptably in situations that he is familiar or experienced with. But, when faced with a new situation or a surprise, he will respond in one of two ways: He may overlook the newness and treat the situation as any other, with a rigid application of existing rules and procedures, whether they are appropriate or not. Or, he may see the newness as a threat and overreact by being too flexible, overly willing to change his approach, and not standing up for the things that do not need to change. In either case, he will not adapt himself effectively to the new reality, causing him to fail to deliver what is needed or even miss an opportunity.

WHY IS FLEXIBILITY IMPORTANT?

The future cannot be precisely predicted. As discussed in "1.5 Continuous Learning," the future work environment will be defined by volatility, uncertainty, complexity and ambiguity (VUCA). People will need to collaborate with others who work in different ways and come from diverse backgrounds, professional experiences and cultures. Achieving success in this environment will require flexibility to respond effectively to unexpected events.

HOW IS FLEXIBILITY LEARNED?

SEE THINGS FROM DIFFERENT PERSPECTIVES

As humans, we are all in the interpretation business. We see something occur, and then we put it through the little machine in our head that makes assumptions, adds meaning based on our own history, and makes a decision on whether what happened is good or bad. We do this automatically, in less than a second. You might call that decision your truth, with a little "t." Of course, everyone else is doing the same thing with their own machines. Author Anaïs Nin said, "We do not see the world the way it is. We see the world the way we are." Once you figure out that your truth is not The Truth, it will be easier for you to see things from different perspectives. Flexibility begins when we suspend our initial judgment and open ourselves to learning more through the search for The Truth.

To help see perspectives, ask yourself a few questions:

- What does this situation mean to me? What is most important to me? Why?

- What would this look like to others involved? What is important to them? Why?

- What would this look like to an outsider, someone who is not involved?

- What is the best way for me to respond to this situation?

Be willing to listen to others nonjudgmentally, without filtering what they are saying through your biased brain. Listen to understand, not to convert, fix or heal. Hear what is important to them, whether you agree or not. Be able to restate their position back to them so well that they would be comfortable letting you represent their position as their advocate. Giving up the need to have everything done "my way or the highway" opens up a flexible world of opportunity. It also gives you new insights into the person you are listening to, and may help you solve the problem you are facing in a new way. When you listen with your heart as well as with your eyes and ears, you learn more. When you learn, new possibilities arise.

TOLERATE NOT KNOWING

Uncertain situations are unpredictable and involve a greater chance of surprises. Ambiguity means that a situation is unclear, opening up a potential for misunderstanding. Clear cause and effect relationships are vague before you start or after you finish. Since uncertainty and ambiguity will continue and increase in the future, learning to treat them as the new normal—to expect the unexpected—will allow you to better deal with what is happening rather than lament about the "good old days."

> **"Only those who will risk going too far can possibly find out how far one can go."**
>
> **– T. S. Eliot, *Transit of Venus***

Randy knew a manager who embraced ambiguity and used to say he could get the most done "when there was dust in the air." At his company, the human resource department responded to financial fluctuations by suspending the managers' ability to recruit new hires. This policy caused added frustration for many managers. Randy's friend kept a list of possible candidates in his top-right desk drawer. It was an active, ongoing list, independent of whether he could hire that day or not. He kept in touch with the people on his list and knew their status. When the hiring light came on, he could act quickly to get great people for his business unit.

TAKE A RISK

Responding to challenges in new ways may feel like a risk. If you define risk as involving possible danger or loss, then, yes, new approaches are risky. However, it is actually riskier to ignore the challenge or deal with a new threat with an outdated mindset and ineffective tools. It reminds us of former Harvard College president

Derek Bok's comment: "If you think education is expensive, try ignorance." If you think change is risky, try not changing.

> **"Life shrinks or expands in proportion to one's courage."**
> **– Anaïs Nin**

As we mentioned in "2.2 Personal Accountability," it is a courageous act to respond to a perceived risk. So, why do it? Because performing a courageous act is the way to develop self-efficacy, grow in your abilities, and get beyond self-imposed borders. People who choose to not take the courageous path may feel safer in the short run, but they will be more vulnerable (taking a bigger risk) in the long term because, by not dealing with the risk, they failed to grow. It might seem contradictory, but if you are worried about risk, take the courageous path.

ADAPT TO CHANGES

To be flexible, you must not only be able to see things differently and recognize the changing circumstances, but also be willing to adapt to changes by solving problems in new ways. Refer to "Part One: Leaders Are Clear Thinkers" for tips on creativity and problem-solving to help you adapt and thrive.

Being flexible does not just apply to the "big things." It also means adapting to changing priorities during your week and day. Meetings, phone calls, flights and other everyday activities are subject to change. By keeping what is really important on track, and being flexible on the other less-critical items, your life will be more pleasant and personally satisfying.

RESILIENCY

WHAT IS RESILIENCY?

Christopher Reeve was an American actor best known for his portrayal of Superman. At the age of 42, at the peak of his physical stature and career, he was thrown from his horse during an equestrian competition. Reeve landed on his head. He did not breathe for the three minutes it took the paramedics to arrive.

When he regained consciousness in the hospital five days later, he found out that the accident had crushed his first two vertebrae. His head was barely connected to his spine. The accident left him permanently in a wheelchair with a breathing apparatus, unable to move a muscle in his body. It would have been easy to give up on life after such an unfair turn of events. He did not.

Instead, until his death nine years later in October 2004, he made his most lasting marks on humanity. His achievements and accolades are too numerous to mention but include producing, directing and starring in films. He wrote two award-winning books. He opened the Christopher and Dana Reeve Foundation Paralysis Resource Center. He lobbied for expanded use of stem cell research. He became a beacon of hope for people with spinal cord injuries, mobility issues and paralysis.

Christopher Reeve chose to be a survivor, not a victim. Because he was already famous before his accident, his circumstance drew publicity, and his case is well-known. Every day, people go through private trials at least as difficult as his and make a similar choice. Maybe they will not be nominated for a Golden Globe award, but they are every bit the resilient survivor that Reeve was.

> "I think a hero is an ordinary individual who finds strength to persevere and endure in spite of overwhelming obstacles."
> – Christopher Reeve

Resiliency is the ability that allows a person to quickly recover from adversity and not quit when he encounters difficulties. A resilient person is persistent, able to cope with problems and setbacks, and continue toward his goals. He deals with a difficult situation objectively and does not personalize it. A resilient athlete, for example, is one who "refuses to lose." He expects to make the winning play. And, when he does lose, he does not let it get him down.

While writing this book, seven-time Wimbledon champion Roger Federer was beat by Sergiy Stakhovsky, ranked 116th in the world, in the second round of the Wimbledon tournament. "It was clearly not what I was hoping for," said the understated Federer. He said he would invoke the "24-hour rule" where you "don't panic" and then "come back stronger." Federer's response shows us that he is resilient—a characteristic of successful, long-lasting athletes.

People who have not yet developed their resiliency may be overwhelmed by a challenge or adversity. They may dwell unnecessarily on a problem, take longer to recover from setbacks, and see themselves as victimized by circumstances. The problem may seem larger, more impactful and longer-lasting than what is likely happening in reality.

WHY IS RESILIENCY IMPORTANT?

As mentioned with other competencies, the future is likely to be even more turbulent than today, with unexpected twists and turns. Some of the unforeseen events will be positive for a given person or cause, and other events will be negative. Being able to deal with whatever the universe throws at you, while keeping focused on a goal, will be a necessary skill to survive and compete in this type of environment.

> "I don't mind you making mistakes; just make new ones."
>
> – U.S. Army Lieutenant-Colonel Jason Cummins

HOW IS RESILIENCY LEARNED?

REMEMBER THAT FAILURE = LEARNING

Setbacks are a normal part of life. How do you typically respond when something negative happens? You have some choice in how you think about and respond to challenges. Although you do not have to smile and yell "Goody!" when something bad happens, you also do not have to say, "Woe is me. Why do bad things always happen to me?" As Napoleon Hill, author of *Think and Grow Rich,* put it: "Every adversity, every failure, every heartache carries with it the seed of an equal or greater benefit." Resiliency is the ability to learn from your mistakes and bounce back with renewed commitment to your vision.

> "[We] never failed to fail. It was the easiest thing to do."
>
> – Jimmy Buffet, "Southern Cross" song lyrics

Thomas Alva Edison, one of the most prolific inventors in the world, is well-known for his persistence in finding a suitable material to use for the filament of his incandescent lamp. He needed one that would glow, not too brightly, and last. He tested carbonized filaments using every wood and plant imaginable. Edison said, "Before I got through, I tested no fewer than 6,000 vegetable growths and ransacked the world for the most suitable filament material." He wrote, "The electric light has caused me the greatest amount of study and has required the most elaborate experiments. I was never myself discouraged, or inclined to be hopeless of success. I cannot say the same for all my associates." During the testing, when someone asked if Edison was discouraged because he had tried so many different things and none had worked, he replied with optimism. He said that he was getting close to an answer because he had already eliminated a lot of the materials that would not work. He saw himself as moving closer to success, rather than experiencing continual failure. The next time something happens that you think is "bad," stop and think about how you can find something good in that event and use it to move forward.

> **"Good mariners are not made on calm seas."**
> **– Proverb**

SEE YOURSELF AS A SURVIVOR, NOT A VICTIM

Resilient people believe they have some control over a problematic situation and have the ability to change it. They see themselves as survivors. Victims believe that a bad event is not their fault and outside their control. Randy was explaining victim thinking during a workshop, and someone who worked in a prison spoke up and said, "That is the language we hear every day from the prisoners. Nothing is ever their fault." When faced with adversity, choose to be a survivor who is developing his emotional strength. Resilience is an emotional muscle that grows stronger as you exercise that choice.

DO NOT LET ONE EVENT HIJACK YOUR WHOLE LIFE

Resilient people remain cautiously optimistic, thinking "this too shall pass" and "I can get through this." They believe setbacks are transient—temporary—and will not affect their whole lives. They do whatever they can in the moment to deal with and localize the problem. If you are dealing with a trial, it is helpful to remind yourself of other parts of your life that are still rewarding and enjoyable.

> "Genius is one percent inspiration and ninety-nine percent perspiration."
>
> – Thomas Alva Edison

STAY FLEXIBLE

Barry Staw of UC Berkeley coined the term "threat rigidity" to describe organizational behavior under threat. In these challenging times, people under stress are more inclined to focus on the one or two things they do well, which narrows their search for any alternative answers to the threat. As you might imagine, this rigidity in decision-making occurs just at the time when flexibility and new thinking is most needed. As we said in the introduction to the last module, flexibility supports resilience. For tips on working on your flexibility, see "2.3 Flexibility."

USE YOUR SUPPORT NETWORK

When faced with a tough problem, having a network of people to talk with and listen to your concerns and ideas is a great help. This network should support your active attempts to stem the effects of the problem. They should not try to solve your problem as they would solve it, nor should they just be sympathetic about how bad things are. Positive support can encourage you to stay engaged with the challenge and actually use the situation to achieve a greater good. The next time you face difficulty, choose people to discuss it with who will help you stay flexible so you can find creative solutions.

A social network can also keep a person engaged in the rest of their life, which helps establish a sense of equilibrium. Friends, family, colleagues and others can encourage someone to continue to exercise, get enough sleep, keep socially engaged, and do the other "normal life" things that can make it easier to deal with a crisis. If you find yourself in such a situation, do not let the problem disconnect you from your support network.

GOAL ACHIEVEMENT

WHAT IS GOAL ACHIEVEMENT?

In March of 2011, Anthony Robles fulfilled a long-time goal. He won the 125-pound class in the NCAA Division I national wrestling championships. As a freshman in high school, Robles had a record of 5-8 and ranked last in the city of Mesa, Arizona. Based on that record, you might think he would decide wrestling was not for him and give up. Instead, he started training intensively and developing new moves based on his body. In his junior and senior years he went 96-0 and won two Arizona state high school wrestling championships. That is an amazing accomplishment, especially considering Anthony Robles was born without a right leg.

Despite being nationally ranked, he was overlooked by the major wrestling colleges, perhaps because of his missing a limb. Instead, Robles chose Arizona State University. In his four years at ASU, he compiled records of 25-11, 29-8, 32-4, and 36-0, again showing his determination and resiliency. The five-feet-eight-inches tall Robles was a three-time PAC-10 conference champion and a three-time NCAA All-American. At the 2011 NCAA meet, he was voted the tournament's Most Outstanding Wrestler, along with another athlete. In July of 2011, he was awarded the prestigious Jimmy V award for Perseverance at the 2011 ESPY awards. And, in January of 2012, he was awarded the 2011 Most Courageous Athlete Award by the Philadelphia Sports Writers Association. Anthony Robles personifies goal achievement. (To watch a video tribute to Anthony, visit our website, www.TheCompleteLeader.org.)

Goal achievement is the ability to execute a plan and get the desired results. The skill relies on self-management and personal account-ability and is aided by flexibility and resiliency. In other words, goal achievement is the end result of leaders leading themselves. A person skilled in goal achievement establishes achievable goals, identifies and implements objectives and activities that will lead to accomplishing the goals, and gets started working toward the goals without undue delay.

> **"True achievers don't run to the finish line; they always run through the finish line."**
>
> **– Ron Price**

Goal achievers have a "can do" attitude. They are realists who see the world as it is and how things work. They approach tasks gladly and quickly. Such people keep focused on progress, can break big projects into manageable smaller chunks, make changes when needed (demonstrate flexibility), and are not easily knocked off course (show resiliency).

People who are not as skilled in goal achievement may be more thinkers or feelers than doers. They may get bogged down in pro-cesses or procedures, taken off track by other people and projects, or distracted by their own wandering interests. These types of people may be easily discouraged when things do not work out as planned. They may be reluctant to start on a project, often thinking they need some other piece of information or action from others before they can move forward. Procrastination stymies goal achievement.

Our friend Bill Bonnstetter is fond of saying, "Doing something is better than doing nothing." Often, by taking the next step, you gain fresh insight or motivation to take another and another; before you know it, procrastination is a fading memory in your rearview mirror.

WHY IS GOAL ACHIEVEMENT IMPORTANT?

A leader can have a compelling vision and an excellent project plan, but until a goal is achieved, the race is not finished. The end result of effective leadership is goal achievement, both personal and in the larger sense.

HOW IS GOAL ACHIEVEMENT LEARNED?

DEVELOP A STRATEGY AND PROCESS

Goal achievement builds on many of the competencies in both "Part One: Leaders Are Clear Thinkers" and "Part Two: Leaders Lead Themselves." In particular, goal achievement requires the skills of futuristic thinking, conceptual thinking, planning and organization, and, often, creativity to establish the goal, plans and milestones to achieve any important result. If you have trouble achieving goals in a timely manner, go back and review your process for completing a goal. Do you follow the same strategy and principles, but modify the implementation, or do you "start from scratch" every time? Leaders must constantly live with paradoxes—competing principles held in tension based on desire outcomes. Sometimes, the failure to achieve is the result of not following proven principles; other times, it is the result of doing the same things over and over again, expecting different results.

Having a strategy and a process for achieving goals will separate you from all the many people who just have a desire to do something, such as lose fifteen pounds. These people typically have some short-term achievement—say, losing five pounds—but give up as progress gets more difficult, only to backslide (for example, putting on ten pounds). In business, you must develop a strategy, based on your vision and mission, to accomplish the organization's goals. Take the same disciplined approach to your personal and professional goals.

We suggested some approaches to solving problems in "1.6 Problem-Solving" and "2.1 Self-Management." For ideas on creating your own process for goal achievement, check those modules. If someone asks you how you achieve goals, you should be able to clearly explain your approach and methodology.

CREATE SMART GOALS

We talked about SMART goals in "1.3 Planning and Organization." We are using the acronym again here, and taking a bit of leeway with the "A" and "R." Use these questions to check your own goals:

- **Specific**: Is the goal clearly and completely stated so it is recognizable when completed?

- **Measurable**: Is there an objective measurement tied to completion? There should be no argument whether or not the stated goal was met.

- **Action-oriented**: What observable behaviors have to be completed to achieve this goal? Think about a behavior or action step that may help achieve the goal. Make a decision and move forward.

- **Realistic**: Is the goal realistic, with a reasonable chance of completion? The goal may be a stretch for your talent or time, with no guarantee of completion, but it should be grounded in reality, not fiction. Hope is not a strategy.

- **Time-bound**: When must this goal be completed? Any goal should have a due date attached to it, in concert with other goals, to complete your overall project on schedule.

Make sure you have large goals broken down into manageable parts with enough checkpoints along the way. Creating SMART goals will help improve your odds of achieving your desired results on time and on target.

MAKE TIMELY DECISIONS

If you have trouble getting started on projects, or hesitate to make needed decisions, review "1.7 Decision-Making." Get feedback on your decision-making style. There are two basic decision-making mistakes: errors of omission and errors of commission. An error of omission occurs when a decision that should be made is not made. Not making a decision—deciding not to decide—is also a decision of sorts. Do you wait until all the facts are in before making a choice? Instead, think about the minimum number of facts that will be required to take the next step.

> "Errors of commission are less damaging to us than errors of omission. ... [Taking] no risk is to accept the certainty of long-term failure."
>
> **– Bob Lutz**

An error of commission occurs when a decision is made incorrectly or should not have been made. If you are working toward a goal, mistakes will be a part of the process. Nobody likes blunders, and we are not recommending a strategy of shooting first and apologizing later. But a bias for action— doing something—is usually better than doing nothing. As we have suggested in other modules, if you make a poor decision, learn from it, reset your goals and plan, and keep moving forward.

PART 3:

LEADERS LEAD OTHERS

A general definition of leadership is well accepted: leaders work through and with their followers to accomplish goals. In Part Three, we look at twelve of the most important competencies needed for getting results through others in an ethical manner. As in Part Two, these competencies are interrelated and support each other.

Consider your own leadership path. Think about all the people that you have influenced or will influence. Reflect on the balance of relationships and results, and you will probably recognize that better results flow from better relationships. The competencies in Part Three are meant to focus on better leading of others, with an emphasis on relationships:

3.1 Empathy – Ability to "see it as they see it" and "feel it as they feel it"

3.2 Understanding and Evaluating Others – Ability to understand others clearly without bias

3.3   Presenting Skills – Ability to communicate ideas effectively with a group verbally

3.4   Written Communication – Ability to articulate a written message in a clear and compelling manner

3.5   Diplomacy and Tact – Ability to treat others fairly

3.6   Interpersonal Skills – Ability to connect with others in a positive way

3.7   Persuasion – Ability to convince others to change their actions, decisions, opinions or thinking

3.8   Negotiation – Ability to constructively facilitate agreements between two or more people

3.9   Conflict Management – Ability to address and resolve the contradictory interests or values of two or more parties in a high emotion, low trust environment

3.10   Teamwork – Ability to work cooperatively with others to achieve group objectives

3.11   Employee Development and Coaching – Ability to facilitate and support the professional growth of others

3.12   Customer Focus – Ability to consistently build long-term relationships based on the delivery of a service, product or other value

In "3.10 Teamwork," we list the four stages of team growth: forming, storming, norming and performing. The leadership relationship often goes through similar phases, and Part Three is organized around these phases. The initial phase, forming, is about communicating, getting to know each other and creating a basic human connection. We connect with and get to know others through an ongoing conversation. Conversations involve both talking and listening, and the ability to listen to and hear others completely and clearly is at the center of leadership. Therefore, we begin Part Three with two listening skills: empathy, and understanding and evaluating others. We follow up those competencies with two skills that leaders use to "talk" to others: presenting and written communication.

As people come together to work on a project, different constituencies attempt to influence each other as everyone tries to find their roles and figure out how to proceed. This is the second leadership phase, storming, which usually includes dealing with differences of opinion. Since effective leaders get along well with others, we have created modules that focus on how leaders connect with those around them: diplomacy and tact, and interpersonal skills.

As storming is worked through, it is replaced by the third leadership phase, norming, which involves getting things done and creating results. Modules on persuasion, negotiation and conflict management explore competencies that will help leaders move their projects forward and get results, particularly when there are roadblocks and disagreements. Each of these skills allows leaders to work with others to overcome what may look like insurmountable barriers to achieving their goals. We also focus on two additional competencies—teamwork, and employee development and coaching—that help a leader get things done through others.

We wrap Part Three up with customer focus. The customer is in a unique class, as they are the group of "others" who decide the value of any product or service. Effective leaders must cultivate a good relationship with their customers so that they understand and provide what customers need—or they risk creating something that no one values or wants. Each of the twelve competencies in

Part Three helps leaders work with others to create results that customers want.

It is sometimes possible to transcend "just getting results" to create something great and lasting. This is the final leadership phase, performing. If you think about leadership relationships, it is probably easy to name groups that transcended simply getting results. For example, the Beatles ("yeah, yeah, yeah"), the U.S. putting a person on the moon ("one small step for man…"), or the Macintosh development team ("90 hours a week and loving it"). Countless other groups, both famous and not, have achieved great results while also creating something special for themselves and the world at large. Opportunity for greatness always exists when people come together to achieve something worthwhile. Part Three is meant to help you develop the skills to encourage greatness.

EMPATHY

WHAT IS EMPATHY?

The word empathy is made up of two parts: em, which means "in," and pathos, which means "feeling." Empathy is the ability to be "in the feeling of the other." When you empathize with someone, you see their experience as they see it and feel it as they feel it. You are able to recognize emotions that another person is feeling. Being empathetic leads to a deeper understanding of others, helping you identify with and care about them.

Empathy is different than simply agreeing with someone else. Instead, it gives the other person the opportunity to become more self-aware of their own feelings and experience. It acknowledges the reality and impact of someone's emotions, without passing judgment.

Empathy is also not sympathy. Sympathy is connecting with someone's feelings because you have experienced something similar. A sympathetic response could be, "I'm sorry for your loss. I know how it is to lose a parent." An empathetic response could be, "My impression is that you feel sad that you lost your father. I'm sure you have fond memories of your time together." You can have empathy without a shared experience.

People who are unable to relate with empathy lack emotional connection with another person. They may not care what the other person is saying, feeling or needing. A person who lacks empathy is quicker to respond with criticism, blame, judgment or an attempt to convince the other person that they are wrong. A lack of empathy may also show up as being disengaged or not caring about the other person or what she is saying. If empathy does not come naturally to you, there are ways to develop this necessary skill.

> "You never really understand a person until you consider things from his point of view ... until you climb into his skin and walk around in it."
>
> – Harper Lee, *To Kill a Mockingbird*

WHY IS EMPATHY IMPORTANT?

Empathy allows people to manage their interpersonal relationships in an authentic way by demonstrating genuine care, respect and understanding for others. Showing empathy builds trust in a relationship. When a person knows she is being listened to, she feels that she matters to the listener. When she feels understood, she tends to relax, feel safer and become more open to hearing other opinions. On the other hand, if she does not feel understood, she will be much less open to hearing different views.

Ron deals with asthma, and he compares the physical feeling of asthma to a lack of empathy. During a conversation, if his airways are constricted and he cannot breathe freely, he is more focused on his own comfort and safety and less interested in what the other person is saying. A shortness of psychological breathing restricts the ability to empathize; empathy, on the other hand, shifts the focus off oneself and on to others, giving another person's ideas psychological "room to breathe."

When leaders create a safe space built on a foundation of trust, they can deal with the "undiscussable" issues that remain below the surface in many organizations—the ones that are only talked about in the "meeting after the meeting." The number of undiscussables that exist in a group or relationship is inversely proportional to the amount of trust that exists. When trust is high, there are few taboos and very little that people cannot talk about openly.

In highly empathetic groups, people listen to and understand the needs of each other. Ideas are freely shared and built upon. Such an environment increases the odds of a robust outcome to problems and solutions that everyone can support. Empathy is the skill that opens the door to better communications and partnership. A person who demonstrates empathy will build authentic and trusting relationships, be better able to effectively deal with difficult issues, and create solutions that everyone can support.

> **"To listen well is as powerful a means of influence as to talk well, and is as essential to all true conversation."**
> **– Chinese Proverb**

Someone who is not skilled at empathy will tend to listen for comments that support her preconceived view of the world and ignore comments that go against that view. This is a very normal, subtle and often unnoticed bias that most of us possess. We tend to confirm our own beliefs instead of setting our own worldview aside temporarily to truly listen to people from their worldview. Our beliefs precede and color our observations. When we fail to empathize, we may believe we understand the other person when, in fact, we do not.

Leaders who lack empathy may appear aloof, distant or insensitive. They will have difficulty understanding the needs and feelings of those around them, so they increase their chances of making decisions that do not incorporate the needs of others. People who do not exhibit empathy tend to say things that sound insulting or inconsiderate, without realizing it. This lack of empathy becomes an interpersonal blind spot.

> "No one cares how much you know,
> until they know how much you care."
> – Theodore Roosevelt

Randy was working through some difficult issues with someone, using the services of a skilled counselor. As he tells the story:

> As we started our conversations, I thought to myself, "I know how to listen with empathy. Shoot, I teach this stuff. I hope the other person wakes up." In fact, I did "know" a lot about empathy, but that did not mean I was practicing it. At some point during this work, the other person's story shifted from my brain to my heart. I felt their pain. And, at that moment, I had two "ahas." One was about what empathy really was. The other, more important, "aha" was about what was really important to the other person.

HOW IS EMPATHY LEARNED?

You may be saying to yourself, "I think I'll skip this next part. I know how to listen." We hope you are right, but if you are, you are in the minority. Very few people are such good listeners that they do not need any improvement. Think about *how* you listen. Can you see others as unique humans and worthy of being listened to? Can you truly set your own ideas and biases aside to hear and understand what they are saying from their points of view?

What is more basic than listening? Many of the skills we learn as children, such as language, are normally learned by listening. Imagine trying to lead any effort without receiving any information from outside your own head. Most of us would agree that is a prescription for failure. In fact, the most effective leaders are careful listeners. They seem to understand what everyone around them is thinking and saying. Here are a few suggestions for improving your empathetic listening:

LISTEN FOR THE RIGHT REASONS

Improving your listening is a learnable skill. As you will find with many leadership competencies, the intention of you, the listener, is critical. If your intention is to get "one up" on the other person, or to use what a person says against him, no amount of skill will help in the long term. But if your intention is to create a bond of trust where authentic communication is the norm—where you can be real with others—the skills will come much more easily. Ask yourself, "What is my true goal as I listen to this other person?"

SUSPEND YOUR ASSUMPTIONS AND BE PRESENT

To listen effectively, you must voluntarily set aside your own views and beliefs—your "mental models" of the world—to hear with empathy. This setting aside is only temporary. You are not giving up anything, except your need to always be right. To listen effectively means to suspend judgment so you can discern the other person's mental models, assumptions, beliefs and feelings. That is the route to understanding another person.

Improved listening, then, develops from the practice of intentional listening. When you first begin listening consciously, you may find it to be hard work. It means paying attention, being present for the other person, and not retracting into your own head while the other person talks. When listening to understand, you are not listening to respond. You are also not listening to judge, convert, fix or heal the other person. That is why you need to temporarily give up your own view of the world, so you can understand how the other person thinks and feels about an issue. One measure of this skill is the ability to state the other person's point of view to his satisfaction, possibly even better than he can.

Most of us are used to doing other things and thinking other thoughts while someone is talking. To really give someone your full attention is quite a nice gift. If you want people to pay attention to you, pay full attention to them.

LISTEN FOR BOTH FACTS AND FEELINGS

Listen to discover the scope, significance and possibility in what the other person is saying. Ask yourself, "How important is this issue to the other person?" "Does the issue affect one part or many parts of their life?" and "How big of a deal is this issue?" After listening for a while, you can check to see if you are in sync with the other person by doing two things:

1. **Summarize facts.** Sum up what the person said by saying, "So what you are saying is [insert summary]" or "If I hear you right you think that [insert summary]. Is that right?"

2. **Reflect feelings.** Show that you understand how the person feels by saying something like, "That makes you feel sad." Say it with a vocal inflection almost like a question to let the other person know you are just checking to make sure you got the right fact or feeling. Many times, the person will say something like, "Well, not sad exactly—more disappointed, I guess."

Randy was working with a group of engineers on the idea of listening for feelings, and he asked them what organs of the body are used to listen. They quickly got "eyes" and "ears." He also gave them credit for "body language" but told them they were still missing an important organ. After pushing and probing, he finally said, "What about listening with your heart?" That is really what listening for feelings is all about. One guy responded, "We're engineers. We don't have hearts; we have blood pumps." "Well then," Randy said, "Let's listen with those blood pumps. "

LISTEN AS A BEGINNER

Effective listening involves acting as a beginner or learner, not an expert. This may be hard for leaders who feel they need to always have the answer. You can practice listening as a beginner by paying attention to someone close to you as if you are hearing them for the first time. This may not be easy, since most of what you "hear" is really your brain filling in the blanks with memories of the person and your own worldview.

> "In my walks, every man I meet is my superior in some way, and in that I learn from him."
> – Ralph Waldo Emerson

If you are practicing this skill with someone you have known for a while, tell him what you want to do. Say something like, "I'm striving to be a better listener. One thing I'm working on is listening to those I care about as if it were our first conversation. Even though I've known you for 20 years, I'm going to try to listen to who you are today, not to my memory of who you were. Okay?"

ASK MORE QUESTIONS

Yet another way to improve your listening skill is to consciously ask more questions and refrain from being the first person to give an answer. Avoid asking a question if you know the answer; that comes across as condescending and does not build trust.

> "The purpose in a man's heart is like deep water, but a man of understanding will draw it out."
> – Proverbs 20:5

You may have to preface this change of behavior with your team. Explain to them, "If we don't get all our brains in the game, we will get beat by companies that better involve the entire team. I'm going to listen more and talk less to try to hear your ideas." Be aware: when someone offers a controversial idea (one you do not like), everyone will watch your reaction. If you revert back to something like, "That won't work" or "We tried that five years ago," that may be the last wild duck idea you get. In the "meeting after the meeting," the team will certainly discuss the contradiction between what you said and did.

We are not saying you should agree with ideas that you have doubts about. But we are saying that responding as a curious learner is better than acting as a judge. Say things like, "Hmm, I hadn't thought of that. Tell me more." Or, "I wonder how that differs from a similar idea we tried five years ago? Who else has a comment or thought on this new idea?"

Even if a suggestion is not your first choice, unless you believe it will do irreparable harm, you may want to let it have life. People tend to work much harder to make their own ideas work.

SERVE OTHERS

Volunteering your time to a nonprofit group is a good way to develop a more empathetic outlook. Serve food, mop floors and do whatever you can to help, without the thought of gaining anything. Then, watch what you gain. Get yourself out of the middle of your own universe. If you do this for a while, you may come to the conclusion that, although separated by circumstances, the differences between you and those you serve are not so great. You will gain compassion as you give compassion. Use this insight in all your leadership.

UNDERSTANDING AND EVALUATING OTHERS

WHAT IS UNDERSTANDING AND EVALUATING OTHERS?

When Randy was in grade school, he had classmates who were "identical" twins. Although they looked very similar, he could easily tell them apart because he was with them every day and knew them well. They obviously had many similarities; but, to someone who knew them well, they were not identical.

Understanding and evaluating others is the ability to see the individuality in others, recognize each person as a unique human being, and understand a person's unique point of view and attitudes. Think of one of your best friends. Do you have any trouble getting him confused with someone else? Probably not, if you are endowed with a normal brain. You can easily create a long list of qualities and quirks that make him who he is. The better you understand another person, the more you can put him in a unique class of one: there is no one else exactly like him.

What about people you meet in another part of the world, where you are perhaps unfamiliar with the language, culture, customs and dress? It may be much harder to describe how each person is different from the other because it can be easier to lump everyone into one large group. You might label them. In this process they become the "other," slightly less human and more like "things."

We do not deny that cultural similarities exist within groups of people. What we are saying is that, underneath those similarities, each individual possesses unique values, experiences and aspirations.

Another part of understanding and evaluating others is the ability to objectively listen to their ideas. You do not have to agree, or even imply agreement, with all their ideas or opinions. It is very possible to understand another person's viewpoint, even to be able to express it as well as he can, and not be in agreement with him. Doing so involves listening to the other person objectively and attentively.

> **"The most basic of all human needs is the need to understand and be understood."**
> **– Ralph Nichols**

The objective listener values all other points of view. She asks for others' thoughts and ideas. She listens to understand the other person's point of view, without bias, using her listening skills of both empathy and understanding others. Evaluating does not equal judging, as in the sense of an annual evaluation. In fact, "evaluating" means unbiased weighing of ideas.

A person who lacks the ability to understand and evaluate others attempts to simplify his world by putting people in groups—sales and manufacturing, Muslims and Christians, introverts and extroverts, Boomers and Millennials, Chinese and Indians. He evaluates people in those groups and their ideas through a biased lens, as if all members are identical. In this case, he will not truly understand, respect and value the diversity of others and their beliefs. This type of person may not properly understand what is required by his manager or why. He may not recognize the distinct talents of his employees or the individual needs of his customers, and this blindness can lead to misjudgments or unacceptable work performance. He may appear to lack interpersonal skills simply because he misinterprets the actions of others. For instance, he might interpret a colleague's comments as disrespectful, when the colleague meant no disrespect at all. Fortunately, this skill can be developed through increased self-awareness and a recognition that deeper understanding almost always leads to greater effectiveness.

WHY IS UNDERSTANDING AND EVALUATING OTHERS IMPORTANT?

Two important aspects of leadership are identifying talents and connecting the right talents to the right job. Many leaders feel they have a great instinct for this. Entrepreneurs we have worked with will often say, "I can tell in the first thirty seconds whether or not a candidate is going to work well in our company." Actually, research indicates that they are correct—about 15 percent of the time. Understanding and evaluating talent is one of the toughest tasks in leadership.

Once a leader understands the unique potential within a person, the next job is to connect those strengths to a position where they will flourish. In his book, *The One Thing You Need to Know: … About Great Managing, Great Leading and Sustained Individual Success*, Marcus Buckingham suggests that great managers believe:

1. Almost everyone wants to do great work.

2. Individuals come to their work with unique and enduring talents that can be productively applied.

3. The best results come from helping people develop their talents into sustainable performance.

Leaders who truly understand others use tools and processes to help team members both identify talents and match their talents to jobs.

In any endeavor of any magnitude, it is impossible for one person to know everything and have all the answers. Success depends on understanding as many views and opinions as possible, so that a project is not blindsided due to a lack of information. Leaders who understand others can more fully access all the ideas, thoughts, feelings, likes and dislikes that reside in their team and will be miles ahead of the competition.

Tomorrow's leaders will need to understand that results flow from relationships in an interdependent, fast-changing world, and that effective relationships cannot exist unless both parties understand each other. This is exponentially more important when leadership involves working across boundaries and cultures, during mergers and acquisitions, or dealing with other situations that will become more complex in the future. People and companies who will thrive will use inclusion and diversity of thought as a competitive advantage. The old adage, "If everyone agrees with each other, they are useless to each other," will prove even truer in tomorrow's world.

HOW IS UNDERSTANDING AND EVALUATING OTHERS LEARNED?

Since understanding and evaluating others is closely linked to empathy, refer to the previous module for ideas and strategies on understanding others. Improving your empathy will improve your ability to understand and evaluate others, and vice versa. Here are some additional ideas:

LOOK FOR MULTIPLE RIGHT ANSWERS

As a developmental exercise, read articles or stories or watch debates that present the same facts through at least two different points of view. Practice identifying with each of the different perspectives. How is each party thinking? What are they feeling? For instance, as we write this book, a current issue in the U.S. is immigration reform. Try to identify with the Republican side, and then try to align with the Democratic side. Do the same for a historical situation that is relevant to your culture. For example, what did the Native Americans think when the first Pilgrims landed at Plymouth Rock? What did the Pilgrims think and feel about the Native Americans? Now, apply this same exercise to a current issue in your place of business or with your family. Attempt to identify with the social perspective of all parties involved.

SOLICIT ALL PERSPECTIVES

When you and your team are considering a decision, insist that all perspectives are stated and understood. Ask those present to do their best to share the outlooks of any missing stakeholders. A useful ground rule is, "You cannot complain after a decision is made if you did not speak up during the deliberation."

> "There are two types of people: those who come into a room and say, 'Well, here I am' and those who come in and say, 'Ah, there you are.'"
> – Frederick Collins

You can also promote this approach by welcoming different perspectives. If someone states a view different than yours, thank them and genuinely do your best to see it from their standpoint before taking issue with their view. Keeping an open mind does not mean giving equal weight to unhealthy ideas such as bigotry or genocide. It does mean doing your best to understand where someone is coming from before responding.

STUDY EMOTIONAL INTELLIGENCE

Author Daniel Goleman wrote about the term emotional intelligence, or EQ, in the 1990s. He identified four basic core elements that make up EQ: self-awareness, self-management, social awareness and relationship management. These are all learnable skills. To better understand others, focus on the social awareness aspect of EQ. (For more on emotional intelligence and an online assessment to measure your EQ, visit www.TheCompleteLeader.org.)

GET TO KNOW PEOPLE

How well do you know those you work with? Do you know the name of their spouses or significant others? Do you know them beyond their present work role? What are their major life accomplishments? What are they interested in outside of work? What do they like to do for fun? Be curious and interested in each person on your team as whole people, not simply employees. Consciously make time for "small talk" which, paradoxically, may be the most important talks you have.

USE A VARIETY OF TALENT PROFILES

As a leader, you are responsible for helping people succeed. As we mentioned earlier in this module, it is important for a leader to accurately understand others so he can identify peoples' unique talents and match those talents to the right positions and projects. Very few leaders can do this well without the aid of talent profiles. The best of these tools creates a picture of a person's natural tendencies, motivators, aptitude and more. Developing a comprehensive understanding of how these profiles should and should not be used will help you gain significant insights into your team members. Talent profiles uncover the unique potentials and challenges for individuals, which allow you to better position people for success. To sample the profiles we use with our clients, go to www.TheCompleteLeader.org.

PRESENTING SKILLS

WHAT ARE PRESENTING SKILLS?

Surveys consistently identify people's top five fears, in order, as: public speaking, death, spiders, darkness and heights. Jerry Seinfeld quipped, "In other words, at a funeral, the average person would rather be in the casket than giving the eulogy." Yet speaking in front of people is key to successful leadership. The ability to communicate verbally with groups involves being able to present ideas effectively. Leaders are people of influence, and one of the primary ways leaders extend influence is by speaking to groups they hope to impact. Whether it is an athletic coach's final words before competition begins, a politician's campaign stump speech, or an executive's presentation to key stakeholders, clear and effective verbal communication has a significant impact on achieving success.

Great presenters organize their thoughts in a logical progression, taking audiences on a journey throughout their presentation. They master the use of stories, metaphors and, depending on the subject or audience, the right dash of humor. Like a great novel or movie, their presentations often follow the time-tested pattern of introducing a topic; presenting and building tension or drama in a manner that rises to a peak of intensity; and concluding with a compelling resolution and call to action.

Everyone has strengths and weaknesses when it comes to speaking to a group. Extroverts have the advantage of verbal skills that have often been honed over a lifetime (because they spend so much time talking). However, extroverts can also overreach and become guilty of exaggeration, pandering and speaking long after their audiences have grown weary from listening.

Introverts normally approach presenting with the advantage of cognitive skills that help their words reflect careful preparation and deeper analysis. On the other hand, their presentations may lack the energy, bodily expressions and auditory inflections that stir the audience to stay engaged and take action. Whatever your presentation style, you can always get better!

When a great presenter finishes talking, the audience feels informed, energized and ready for action. Such presenters invest time and effort into understanding their audiences, are clear about their objectives, and focus their presentations on achieving those goals. This is in contrast to good, mediocre or poor speakers who often think that the purpose of their presentation is to impress others with self-promotion or pure entertainment.

Presenting is not about you. It is about adding value to the people in your audience. Communicating ideas effectively is an achievable and worthy goal for any leader.

WHY ARE PRESENTING SKILLS IMPORTANT?

All leaders are accountable to someone. Whether a board of directors, a senior leadership team, an electorate or a regulatory body, leaders have the opportunity to communicate results and plans, and to expand and solidify their influence through presentations. Dale Dixon, a friend of Ron's, is regularly hired to coach corporate leaders on their presentation skills. Dale starts his training by showing his clients what *not* to do. Over the years, he has collected a vast library of videos, audio recordings and digital presentations that vividly demonstrate how quickly a leader's credibility is damaged through poor preparation, simple mistakes in voice or body language, or ineffective visual aids.

Time and again, Dale's work results in his clients becoming better presenters. They obtain new resources, achieve substantial promotions, and more effectively respond to crises or media opportunities. Effective presentations lead to improved leadership results.

HOW ARE PRESENTING SKILLS LEARNED?

LOOK FOR OPPORTUNITIES TO PRESENT

As with every new skill, presenting is mastered through practice, practice and more practice. One of the greatest opportunities available today for developing presenting skills is to join Toastmasters International (www.toastmasters.org). Founded in 1924, Toastmasters is a nonprofit educational organization dedicated to teaching speaking and leadership skills in more than 14,350 chapters in over 122 countries. Members meet weekly to help each other become more confident and competent in front of an audience.

Ron's son, Daniel, was named Young Entrepreneur of the Year in 2010 by the U.S. Small Business Administration. As a result, he started receiving invitations from across the country to come and tell his story. Though he had taken a public speaking course in college, he called and asked Ron for a book he could read to improve his speaking skills. Ron's response was, "Unless you plan to become a professional speaker and give hundreds of speeches each year, there isn't that much you need to focus on in order to be effective." Instead, Ron gave him the following list of five things to keep in mind:

HAVE A POWERFUL PRESENCE AND BE AUTHENTIC

Ron was asked to coach an emerging leader in a multibillion-dollar company. The senior executive who hired Ron explained that his up-and-coming leader was smart, thoughtful and dedicated. However, she struggled with making presentations to boards and committees, often starting with a strong voice and ending with a whimper. He explained that she did not seem to have the "executive presence" that she would need to rise to the highest echelons of leadership in the company.

In working with this high potential executive, Ron discussed "presence" by offering her four different concrete ideas that might help you, too:

- First, he challenged her to dress for work each day as if she were going to an interview for a CEO position.

- Next, Ron expanded on that idea by encouraging her to think of every conversation as a simulation for her interview to become the next CEO of her current company, with everyone she spoke with having a vote (regardless of their current title, role or level of authority). This helped her develop an executive presence no matter who she was meeting with or the topic of conversation.

- Then, Ron asked her if her office looked as she would want it to appear if the President of the United States were to stop by today. If not, he told her, "Get and keep it that way at once!"

- Finally, Ron asked her to significantly "up her game" as an engaged participant when others were presenting, no matter how small or large the audience.

Why did he give this advice, when none of these practices were directly related to her presentations? The answer is simple: a great presenter is not simply putting on a new face when she stands before a group. Instead, she is extending her leadership influence into a new, more powerful arena. If she can create a stronger leadership presence on a daily basis, this will shine through with much more authenticity when the spotlight turns to her. In addition, this practice is one of the most successful tactics for overcoming stage fright. The more you believe you belong in front of a group, the clearer you are about what you are going to say, the easier it will be to relax and deflect the butterflies in the stomach most people experience. Your audience also tends to give you more respect based on your interactions with them when you are not presenting, and this will translate into positive energy coming from the audience toward you, helping you relax under the spotlight. Practicing Ron's "behind the scenes" recommendations daily builds presenting skills, and the easier and more natural speaking becomes.

> **"Every point needs to have a story, and every story needs to have a point."**
> **– Charlie "Tremendous" Jones**

When you stand in front of an audience, focus on authenticity. If you become an actor and attempt to be someone or something that you are not, you immediately lose power. To be authentic, never accept an invitation to speak about something you do not know or care about. Also, do not begin your presentation with someone else's joke, particularly if you do not bring a natural and discerning sense of humor! An ill-timed and poorly-delivered joke—especially one someone in the audience already heard from someone else—is the surest way to destroy authenticity. Instead, if you want to start with a story, whether humorous or not, make it compelling and make it your own.

This may seem obvious, but do not steal other presenters' materials. If you use someone else's expertise, give him or her credit (especially if it is a team member attending your presentation). Not acknowledging that you are borrowing content from someone else is one of the quickest ways to lose credibility as a presenter *and* leader.

PREPARE IN ADVANCE

Prepare your speech in advance, with a focus on the clarity of your message (logic), the conviction of your heart (passion), and how the audience will be attracted to your message (because attraction is more powerful than persuasion). To achieve clarity, keep it simple and avoid trying to say too much. To express conviction, find something to speak about that you believe in strongly. To create a presentation that attracts others, do not give your audience reasons to reject your message because of a flawed style.

Do not think about the mechanics of your presentation while you are "live." Focus on the audience and your message. Practice the mechanics as much as necessary to become comfortable prior to the presentation, then forget about them once the "curtain is raised."

ELIMINATE SLOPPY SPEECH, MOVEMENTS AND APPEARANCE

Avoid actions, clothing, accessories and words that take the focus off of your message. Before taking the stage, look in the mirror and ask the critical question: "Will anything detract from the message or distract the audience?" Inspect for flashy jewelry, name tags, bent collars, loose change in the pocket, gum or unzipped trousers.

Sloppy speech, such as using the phrases "you know," "like," and repetitive "ums" distract and potentially irritate your audience. Similarly, every motion should have a motive. Pacing back and forth without a clear "stage presence" may help you relax, but it detracts from your power and presence. Idiosyncrasies, such as twitching, rising on your toes and then falling back down on your heels, swiveling in a chair, and holding onto the lectern also cause your presentation to lose focus and authority. If you use physical expressions, whether with the face, hands or arms, or more dramatic expressions, match the size of your body language to the size of your audience. For example, opt for a more muted style in the boardroom and larger-than-life movements on the stage at Radio City Music Hall.

SPEAK DIRECTLY TO YOUR AUDIENCE

Talk to those seated farthest away from you to ensure everyone can hear you. Maintain eye contact with several key people throughout the audience throughout your presentation. Master the art of speaking to individuals while addressing your entire audience. Do not look to the floor or ceiling while you are speaking, which communicates nervousness, boredom or laziness as a presenter.

MANAGE THE TECHNICAL DETAILS

Technical details matter. Using a microphone is one more step to being sure your message is heard, so learn to be comfortable with one. Always test a sound system (as well as other technologies you will use) before your audience arrives. Whenever possible, make sure there is adequate lighting on you as the speaker and, whenever the group is larger than thirty people, request an elevated stage. These technical matters have a significant impact on how close and connected your audience will feel. If something goes wrong (and if you present very often, it will), do not worry about it or keep apologizing. Acknowledge what is necessary and move on.

If you use visual aids, such as digital slides or images, use them sparingly and learn the best practices so that these tools enhance rather than detract from your presentation. This point about the use of visual aids seems to be a given, yet it is one of the greatest travesties we continue to see from many presenters who should know better. In addition, realize that the more technology you include, the more prepared you need to be if the technology fails.

> "You tell 'em what you are going to tell 'em, then you tell 'em, then you tell 'em what you told 'em."
> –Edward R. Murrow, legendary broadcaster

Two final thoughts on presenting: Do not expect everyone to love you. Everybody will not; that is impossible. So, do not worry about it. The more time you spend in the spotlight, the thicker your skin will need to grow. Once you have overcome the fear of presenting, and start to enjoy the opportunity to speak to and influence others, be careful not to enjoy it too much. Speakers who fall in love with their speaking tend to start using "I" too much and tend to linger too long on the platform, prompting their audiences to begin wondering how much longer they'll go before they will finish. The greatest presenters always leave their audiences with a clear picture of "what is next" and a lingering desire for more.

WRITTEN COMMUNICATION

WHAT IS WRITTEN COMMUNICATION?

Written communication began in ancient times, with pictographs chiseled into stone. It later progressed to alphabets and language written on animal skins, then paper. With the invention of movable type in 1440, Gutenberg unleashed a revolution of written communication that has continued today and has exploded into the digital world. E-mail and social media are now major forms of communication and will be even more so for tomorrow's leaders.

Written communication is the ability to articulate a message in a clear and compelling manner. Someone who is skilled in written communication knows his audience, has a clear purpose and provides just the right quantity of words, arranged masterfully to achieve his purpose. Someone who is not yet skilled in written communication may use the wrong word, misspell words or use incorrect grammar. He may not have a clear purpose for his communication or be able to clearly articulate his message. He may also make the communication unnecessarily long—or not long enough. While a person who has not yet mastered written communication will not write in a clear and concise manner, this is a skill that can be developed with practice.

WHY IS WRITTEN COMMUNICATION IMPORTANT?

Written communication has great power to produce positive results or cause great harm. In today's connected world, there are more opportunities than ever to write, even if the message is only as long as a social media update. Every phrase or sentence carries significant weight, partially because of how widely and quickly it can spread.

All writing that is disseminated goes to a reader who interprets it through filters of understanding and bias. Considering the broad spectrum of these filters and the uniqueness of each individual's experiences, no message conveyed in writing is ever received exactly as intended. Therefore, your challenge as a writer is to write as clearly and thoughtfully as possible, with the hope of minimizing the degree of misunderstanding or unintended emotional response from readers.

Randy has a friend who managed employees and contractors in Hong Kong, Ireland and the Philippines from her office in Kentucky. Weekly phone conversations and occasional visits helped develop and maintain the relationships among them. However, because of different time zones, most communication was written. Clear writing was the cornerstone of successful results in that global environment.

A few years ago, Ron received an e-mail from someone in South Africa who had just read a novel Ron coauthored more than a decade earlier. This person wrote to him that her life was changed as a result of reading his story. Similarly, Ron still receives requests annually for a play script he wrote back in the late seventies. Even though Ron modestly says both works were far from perfect, they are excellent examples of why we should never undervalue the innate possibilities unleashed by the written word.

HOW IS WRITTEN COMMUNICATION LEARNED?

Even prominent leaders are intimidated by the challenges of written communication, so if this is a difficulty for you, you are not alone. Maybe old, emotional experiences of red markings on school assignments have anchored this lack of confidence into many people's psyches. Whatever the reason, the possibilities for expanding your influence through the written word are too great to ignore.

LEARN THE BASICS

Learn and follow the basic rules of punctuation, grammar and spelling. Unless you are writing poetry or fiction, deviation from the basic rules is not an expression of personality. Instead, it communicates a lack of discipline and respect for the written word.

One of the best ways to develop skill as a writer is to read often. Read with the intention of learning more about the art and skill of writing. What makes great writing effective? What bothers you about poor writing? Whatever the genre, from social media updates to reports, learn by studying the writing of others.

> **"Let me live, love and say it well in good sentences."**
> **– Silvia Plath, novelist, poet and short story writer**

In addition to reading, take a class in writing at your local community college or university, or online. Consider hiring a writing coach to work with you one-on-one. Though this requires a commitment you may consider too great, it is a wise investment in your future. Focus on the style of writing that will best advance your career aspirations, whether business writing, creative writing or another genre.

Focus, also, on continually building your vocabulary. The Johnson O'Connor Research Foundation has proven that one of the clearest predictors of future earnings and influence is the breadth and depth of a person's vocabulary. A good tool for building vocabulary is a site like www.freerice.com, which donates rice to the hungry for each correct answer. There are also apps for smartphones and tablets that provide daily vocabulary words. The key is not just studying but intentionally using the vocabulary you learn in your daily interactions. For more ideas, visit our website, www.TheCompleteLeader.org.

THINK BEFORE YOU WRITE

Before getting started, make sure writing is the best approach and most appropriate response or action, and that you are the right person to respond. Quickly ask yourself a few questions:

- Would this be better answered person-to-person?
- Is this topic so complex that discussion would be more efficient and effective instead?
- Is this a "hot button" or emotional subject to you or the other person (see "3.9 Conflict Management" for more on this topic)?
- Is the issue urgent? Would a phone call solve it more quickly?
- Is this problem really yours to solve? Or, should you delegate it to someone in your organization or send it to the appropriate peer? If so, politely acknowledge the problem and send it along.

KNOW YOUR AUDIENCE

Always write with a clear purpose in mind. Create and keep an index card in front of you as you write that includes the following:

- Who is my audience, and who else should I expect will read this?
- What do I want to accomplish through this communication?

- What do I want the reader to learn, decide or do as a result of reading this?
- Is this informative, do I hope to influence and persuade, or am I simply writing to entertain?
- What is the best style to use for my intended audience?

When considering the behavioral styles, motivations and culture of your primary reader(s), your topic, purpose and audience may require that you are:

- brief, specific and to the point;
- inspirational, friendly or humorous;
- logical, balanced, sympathetic and contemplative; or
- detailed, analytical and fact-driven.

It is also useful to learn to communicate effectively with people who have a different native language from you (both written and verbal). This might mean writing to someone who speaks English as a second language, or it can also include learning and practicing another language yourself. Often, communicating with those who did not learn English as their native language helps identify many colloquialisms that can be confusing or easily misunderstood.

After writing, check for jargon. Are you using phrases that might not translate clearly? Finally, just because someone else speaks English does not mean they speak the same English as you do. One obvious example is the way different generations use different vocabulary, often feeding into the generation gaps that have repeated themselves over and over again.

MAKE ALL YOUR WRITING IMPORTANT

Ron knew and worked with Og Mandino, the author of *The Greatest Salesman in the World* which has sold over 30 million copies since it was first published in 1968. Og told Ron that he agonized over every word, phrase, sentence and paragraph in his writing, sometimes taking months to complete one chapter of 3,000 words. Og respected the power of the written word. He considered his writing a permanent and transparent record of his values, expertise and character.

> "Only half of writing is saying what you mean.
> The other half is preventing people from reading
> what they expected you to mean."
>
> – James Richardson

Like Og, give all writing importance. Write as if everything you write, from an e-mail to a full-length book, will eventually end up in the public domain. Do not write something that you are not willing to read in the newspaper, defend in court, or have sent to any friend, colleague, competitor or family member. Do not use any language, tell stories or pass along jokes you would not send to your mother—assuming your mother represents dignity, poise and moral integrity.

Also, think before hitting "send." Do not fill the e-mail inboxes of others with unnecessary carbon copies (cc) of "thanks" or trivial responses. The rule to remember is, "If it won't benefit them, don't send it."

Make sure, too, that anything you write is clear, concise, compelling and correct. The likelihood that someone will read your writing will often be in direct proportion to the number of words (or lack thereof) and your reputation as an effective writer. Most word-processing software includes spelling and grammar check. Use it. Edit and proofread everything you write. If it is an important piece of writing, ask someone else to proofread it, also. What gets inspected keeps getting better. Be tough on yourself when it comes to following the basic rules of spelling, grammar and punctuation. In business writing, the most important items to get right are the names of people and companies; there is no quicker way to create resistance to your intended purpose than those types of misspellings.

To increase the impact of your writing, look for opportunities to add pictures, graphics or other visual accouterments. Of course, always fit these to the genre you are writing for and only use them to illuminate or increase your impact.

Perfection is not attainable. But, the higher your standards, the more influence your writing will have, as long as it is timely and you are not abdicating other responsibilities to focus solely on writing. Although you should be tough on yourself, be patient and forgiving of the shortcomings of others (unless they have asked you for feedback or mentoring). Look beyond any deficiencies and respond based on their best intent.

> "Tomorrow is the first blank page of a 365 page book.
> Write a good one."
> **– Brad Paisley**

FOLLOW A PROCESS

All writing, no matter how long or how short, follows a process. For most, this includes: draft, edit, rewrite. It is a tidy Plan-Do-Check-Act cycle. For longer pieces, plan by jotting notes and brainstorming. You might need to write an outline to help you plan, as well. Experiment and develop a process that works best for you, then use it consistently to enhance your writing productivity.

Try to write quickly and in your own words. Be authentic. Go back and review or edit your writing, and revise to clarify, cut and add. When you are comfortable with it, send it. This process can take from three minutes to three years, depending on what you are doing. Just remember that it is a process, and most anybody can do it.

DEAL WITH CONFLICT CAREFULLY

Resist the temptation to use written communication as a means to address interpersonal conflict, unless you are documenting or confirming previous verbal communication. It has been estimated that words and content make up only 7 percent of the meaning transmitted in face-to-face communication. The other 93 percent is made up of factors such as body language and tone of voice. And, since those factors are missing in written communication, words are interpreted by the readers in their own voice. In cases of conflict, there are far too many minefields of potential misinterpretation or emotional hijacking to depend on written communication as an effective conflict manager—particularly with the digital communication forms we use today such as texting, status updates and e-mails.

If you must address conflict or performance issues in writing, it is good practice to never send the document the same day as you write it. A good night's sleep will often help clarify your thinking and calm your emotions. This time delay also applies if you are considering responding to antagonistic e-mails, status updates, texts or other writing. If you are writing about a controversial subject, write a draft and review it carefully. Ask a peer to read it before you send it. Remember, once you post an update or hit "send," your written words have become a permanent record of the digital universe.

WRITE CONSISTENTLY

Write something creative every day. Whether journaling, writing poetry to your loved ones, or working on a work-related project, set aside some time to write beyond the demands of the workplace.

Start—and continue writing—your autobiography. One of the disciplines of great writers is they do not write about topics they are ignorant about. This means that research is a critical part of professional writing. If you start by writing about yourself, there is a good chance your expertise will be unmatched!

Joining or forming a writing group can also be helpful. Why not work on your writing with others, whether inside your company or among a broader group of friends? Peer accountability, encouragement and coaching will accelerate your skill development.

BE AUTHENTIC

Communicating by writing is a divergent problem, not a convergent one; there is no one "perfect" solution and almost no such thing as "perfect" writing. So, keep high standards but let go of the idea that your writing will ever be completely perfect.

Instead, aim for authenticity. Give deep thought to what you want to say, especially if you are writing about a complex topic. Write in simple language; do not strive to "sound" a certain way, or to impress somebody. Be polite, give the subject the depth of thought it deserves, and trust yourself to convey your meaning to others.

3.5

DIPLOMACY AND TACT

WHAT ARE DIPLOMACY AND TACT?

In his memoir, *A Journey: My Political Life,* former British Prime Minister Tony Blair writes about efforts to achieve a negotiated agreement with several opposing parties in the Northern Ireland conflict. It was a complex situation: there were not just two groups with opposite objectives; there were several competing groups on both sides of the issue. The ability to listen carefully to understand all the concerns, and then to carefully craft his words to move all groups toward a common goal, was a masterful demonstration of diplomacy and tact by Blair, chief negotiator George Mitchell, and the other mediators involved.

Diplomacy and tact are the ability to treat others fairly, in a sensitive and effective way, regardless of personal biases or beliefs. People who have a well-developed sense of tact and diplomacy are usually polite and courteous. They choose their words carefully to avoid unnecessarily arousing hostility. Diplomatic and tactful people use appropriate discretion and work to build understanding.

People who have not yet developed tact and diplomacy may have reputations for being harsh, blunt or rude. They may intimidate others and focus mainly on results and not on the people or the process. These untactful people may describe their behavior as "results-oriented" or "direct." People may say about them that "you always know what they are thinking," as a way to put a positive spin on their behavioral style.

We are not advocating being unnecessarily indirect, political or "soft." One hallmark of effective leaders is that they can be respectful toward people while being hard on issues. We *are* advocating a mature balance between results and relationships. It is certainly possible to be both sensitive and direct. For example, we learned of a situation where an excellent leader called an employee into his office and fired her. Even though she had just been let go, the employee thanked the leader for treating her fairly, in spite of the outcome. This leader was sensitive, tactful and honest. Part of this skill of mastering tact is to be able to discern how direct to be in any given situation.

As J.G. Randall, Civil War historian and Lincoln scholar, explained, "Tact is a number of qualities working together: insight into human nature, sympathy, self-control, a knack of inducing self-control in others, avoidance of human blundering, readiness to give the immediate situation an understanding mind and a second thought. Tact is not only kindness, but kindness skillfully extended."

WHY ARE DIPLOMACY AND TACT IMPORTANT?

Tomorrow's leaders will be working with a diverse combination of people, not only in their own organization, but also with individuals around the world. Diplomacy and tact maintain positive relationships with others by treating them fairly and with respect.

They allow others to save face. These skills help to bridge differences between people, such as diversity in race, national origin, religion, gender, lifestyle, age and disability.

> "Tact is one of the first mental virtues; the absence of it is fatal to the best talent."
> – William Gilmore Simms

Tact and diplomacy are also two of the skills that underpin interpersonal skills. Being diplomatic and tactful helps you see who another person is and appreciate him, if for no other reason than he is human. As humans, people are worthy of our respect, and they deserve to be treated fairly. Of course, this does not mean that leaders must agree with or even put up with another person's point of view or behavior. If there is a disagreement, a person practicing tact and diplomacy is able to "disagree without being disagreeable."

A leader who practices diplomacy and tact realizes that innovation and creativity develops from differences—new and different ways of seeing the same thing. If everyone on a team views all problems and solutions the same way, they are useless to each other. An effective team needs people to represent different factions, ideas and positions involved. Differences can either create synergy or chaos; synergy can result if differences are respected and valued. When all positions are heard, a more complete and lasting decision can be made.

As we discussed in "3.1 Empathy," over time a team that practices diplomacy and tact with each other will create a level of trust and respect where members feel safe enough to bring up their toughest issues—even issues that might put themselves in a bad light. They will do this because they know the information will not be used against them by other team members. They also know it is more important for the good of the organization to deal with all problems quickly than to hide problems or create "undiscussables."

HOW ARE DIPLOMACY AND TACT LEARNED?

ALIGN YOUR IMPACT WITH YOUR INTENTIONS

When we do dialogue workshops, we often say, "There are two experts in every conversation. I am the expert of my intent. You are the expert of my impact." Diplomacy and tact are about how you say what you need to say. Most of the meaning in communication is not conveyed by the words we choose. It is conveyed in our unspoken body language and demeanor—*how* we say those words.

> "Tact is the art of making a point without making an enemy."
> – Sir Isaac Newton

We have all heard of the Golden Rule: "Do unto others as you would have them do unto you." The Platinum Rule states, "Treat others the way they want to be treated." You can improve diplomacy and tact by being aware of how others' actions affect you and thinking about how your actions will be received. Think before you speak. Ask yourself, "What will be the impact of my communication, including words, tone of voice and body language?" and "What meaning am I conveying?" To align your impact with your intentions, consider these ideas:

- Use your listening skills to help you better understand what is important to the other person.

- Learn more about emotional intelligence so you can manage your communication (words, tone, body language, timing) in a way that encourages trust and cooperation. (Visit www.TheCompleteLeader.org for more on emotional intelligence, including an EQ assessment.)

- Try holding back your own opinions until you understand the other person. In the words of author Dr. Stephen R. Covey, "Seek first to understand, then be understood."

- Watch people you know who seem to have a sense of tact and diplomacy. Notice the words they use and how they often present questions instead of arbitrary statements. Pay attention to how they confront problems objectively, with respect. Can you adapt your behavior to be more like them, while maintaining your authenticity?

BE SELF-AWARE

As with several of the other leadership talents, it is important for you to know what you want to accomplish and compare that to what is actually happening, in as close to real time as possible. That means you need to be "present" and aware of what you are saying and doing, as well as how it appears to be received by the other person. Being self-aware is a key component of emotional intelligence.

If there is a gap between what you hoped to accomplish and the response or results you are getting, you can attempt a correction. The correction may start with evaluating how what you said was perceived by the other person. If the perception is negative, perhaps a quick apology is in order.

ASK FOR FEEDBACK

Most of us have behavioral blind spots that keep us from being as effective as we could be, which is why getting honest feedback from a coach, mentor or trusted peer can be of benefit. People in your organization may not feel comfortable giving you negative feedback, particularly if you are higher up the ladder of hierarchy. However, if you share specifically with them that you are working to develop more diplomacy and tact, and then ask for specific feedback about specific situations, there is a much higher likelihood you will build the trust that gives them the courage to share their observations. Feedback from others, if it is well-intentioned and acted upon, can greatly speed up your progress.

Randy was working with a manager to help get ready for a coaching conversation with one of the manager's employees. As they practiced the situation, with Randy as employee, the manager spoke the correct words, but his body language was very aggressive. He sat on the edge of the chair, his jaw tight and body rigid. As they discussed what was happening, the manager realized how irritated he felt about the employee's work, but he knew he had not done a good job of giving the employee feedback in the past. Now, it was difficult for the manager to have this coaching conversation without blaming or judging the employee.

Randy suggested that the manager take a deep breath, pretend he was having this conversation with one of his friends, and try again. The manager's body language changed, and the impact of his conversation became much different and more effective. Without this outside feedback, it would have been difficult for the manager to understand or adapt his communication for a positive impact.

INTERPERSONAL SKILLS

WHAT ARE INTERPERSONAL SKILLS?

Interpersonal skills are a set of talents that help someone connect with others in a positive manner; the term applies to a cluster of more basic "relating" skills. This skill set is comprised of other competencies we have already talked about, including empathy, understanding and evaluating others, and diplomacy and tact. Since interpersonal skills are practiced in social situations and conversations with others, a person talented in this area knows how to both listen to and speak to others effectively. Such people are also both self-aware and sensitive to others. They are polite and knowledgeable, do not prejudge others, and see people as interesting and unique.

People who have not yet mastered interpersonal skills tend to misunderstand others and either overestimate or underestimate their own capabilities. This set of personal talents also comes more naturally to some than others. For instance, a naturally outgoing, optimistic person may find it easier to initiate and develop business relationships than a more introverted person. However, once a more introverted leader understands the importance of initiating, developing and nurturing relationships, he can adapt his natural behavior to the needs of the situation.

WHY ARE INTERPERSONAL SKILLS IMPORTANT?

Interpersonal skills enable a person to successfully work with a wide range of individuals at varying levels of an organization. Effective interactions build rapport and create clear, consistent, considerate and understandable communications. As a result, it is easier to relate to and work cooperatively with a diverse range of people of varying backgrounds, ages, experiences and education levels.

> "The most important single ingredient in the formula for success is knowing how to get along with people."
> – Teddy Roosevelt

Effective leaders in tomorrow's world will understand that results, both good and bad, flow from relationships—and interpersonal skills are critical to creating long-lasting relationships. They will know that the best and brightest people want to work where they are acknowledged as unique and valuable humans, where they are listened to and their opinions matter. Tomorrow's leaders will also know that wisdom lies within others, not only in themselves. Good interpersonal skills help leaders involve their teams in creating positive results.

Although people often get hired based on their expertise and "hard" skills, what limits their growth and leadership potential is more often the "soft" skills. Daniel Goleman, one of the pioneers of the concept of emotional intelligence (EQ), has said that EQ has a profound impact on leadership effectiveness. In fact, both EQ and IQ are needed for the most effective leadership. But the ability to connect with others in a positive way is one of the "must have" skills a leader needs to influence, develop and coach others, and do well in a broad range of situations.

HOW ARE INTERPERSONAL SKILLS LEARNED?

By definition, interpersonal skills involve working with other people. You can work on developing these talents by working with a trusted friend or coach, but you can also improve on your own. Following are some ideas for developing interpersonal skills:

MANAGE YOUR ONLINE SELF

In our increasingly connected world, where you are constantly "online"—even when you are not on your computer or smartphone—interpersonal skills are always exposed, for better or worse. Your ability to connect with others is reflected in how you engage with others on social media platforms.

Branding and strategic marketing expert Justin Foster, one of our associates, explains that interactions through social media should reflect the real you. If you are engaged, funny or insightful in person, this is what you should express through your status updates, messages and blogs. If you see the value of separating personal and professional conversations, you should manage your online "friends" and "connections" accordingly.

COLLECT COINS

Justin has helped several of our clients develop targeted potential contact lists that he refers to as "Circles of Influence" (COINS). He suggests that not all relationships are equal, and you can define the strength of a relationship and its connectivity with the rest of the world. Under relationship rankings, from strongest to weakest, he includes:

1. Close friends
2. First-name basis
3. Casual or business-only friendships
4. People you have met

5. People you know of but have not been introduced to

Justin ranks how people are "connected" to the rest of the world as follows:

1. National or global

2. Local "connector"

3. Locally well-known

4. Strong networker

5. Not enough data to know

The point of Justin's advice is that there is a structural aspect to managing your relationships. Create a system to help you with this part of your leadership, and it will improve your ability to form and grow effective relationships. Whether on a spreadsheet or online CRM (customer relationship management) software, build and maintain a list of the people you know. Rank the strength of your relationship and their degree of influence. Nurture and build mutually beneficial relationships. Explore ways you can support your high scoring COINS and give them opportunities to support your projects and goals.

FORM A CONNECTION

Ron teaches a simple technique for making connections that he calls FORM. When you meet someone, remember to discuss:

Family: Ask questions about a new acquaintance's family.

Occupation: Ask questions about the person's current and/or past career experiences.

Recreation: Ask what this person enjoys doing outside of work.

Mission: Ask questions to find out what matters most to this person.

When you use this formula with a genuine desire to get to know others, you will create meaningful connections. FORM far surpasses the artificial practices of exchanging business cards while sizing up whether the other person is a potential supplier or customer.

CREATE FORMAL AND INFORMAL INFLUENCE

Organizational researchers are studying the impact of informal influence, defined as influence that is earned through interpersonal skills. This is in contrast to the more well-known formal influence, driven by position. Be aware of the influence of both personal connections and position in your leadership.

In *The Hidden Power of Social Networks: Understanding How Work Really Gets Done in Organizations*, author Robert Cross outlines four specific ways you can build informal influence. Cross identifies both functional and emotional connections. Similarly, the Reya Group (www.reyagroup.com) developed four questions that help build a map of interpersonal relationships in an organization. You can use these four questions to assess your own, or another person's, informal influence.

There are two functional connection questions:

1. From whom do I typically get work-related information?

2. To whom do I regularly go for expert advice or knowledge?

And two emotional connection questions:

1. Whom do I feel energized by when I interact with them?

2. With whom am I completely comfortable sharing my ideas and opinions?

You can also ask these four questions in reverse. For example: "Who comes to me regularly for work-related information?" This will help you assess your own informal influence.

BALANCE ASKING, TELLING AND AFFIRMING

The speaking part of a conversation mostly involves either asking a question or making a statement. But a powerful yet little-used conversational tool, affirming, can enrich discussions and strengthen interpersonal relationships. We consider affirming as making a positive statement about others.

> "Arguing with a fool proves there are two."
> – Doris M. Smith

At work, what percentage of your conversation is advocacy (making statements and arguing for your own ideas) and what percentage is inquiry (asking a question)? You probably have attended staff meetings where few questions, if any, were asked. Take a minute and think about these "advocacy face-offs," and you will recognize that they are more about ego than learning. Asking a question gives the other person psychological space or freedom in the conversation. It allows him to take the conversation in a new direction if he wants to. Effective leaders tap into all the ideas and meaning available in the heads and hearts of all involved. They harness the "wisdom of the crowd" not through making speeches but by asking good questions.

Along with inquiry, affirmation is an important part of building strong relationships. From Blanchard's and Johnson's classic *The One Minute Manager* to the relatively new field of positive psychology and appreciative inquiry, there is growing evidence that focusing on what you and others are doing well, and why it is working, opens up valuable conversations that build strong relationships and meaningful results. This is the affirmation part of the conversation.

Leaders who have mastered interpersonal skills are effective at all three aspects of the speaking side of conversations: asking, telling and affirming. When you apply these skills with authenticity and the right intention, without aiming to mislead or manipulate, you build strong relationships. Since this type of skill-building requires two or more people, consider working on having affirmative conversations with a friend or accountability partner.

CREATE SAFETY AND HIGH TRUST

As mentioned, conversations involve more than just asking questions. In the most effective environments, people are willing to state their opinions, even if those views differ from the group or their boss. This happens because they feel safe to do so, and they trust that what they say will not be used against them. Trust in a relationship is bidirectional; you need to give it to get it. Trust is not built immediately. Instead, it takes time to create a trusting relationship. However, once it is built, a high-trust connection is a tremendous competitive advantage.

What are you, as a leader, doing or not doing to make it safe for people to state opinions—even unpopular ones? If you are not actively working to build a high-trust environment, your organization may get blindsided by something that was known but not voiced to the appropriate leaders.

A horrible example of failure to communicate critical facts is the Challenger spacecraft disaster in January 1986. The Rogers Commission Report indicated that the direct cause of the accident was O-ring failure due to cold outdoor temperature. During the reviews after the accident, it became apparent that a number of engineers and project managers knew that the O-rings could become brittle at a low temperature and could cause a disaster. The U.S. space program at the time was under severe pressure to make its launch dates and, in this case, bad news about the O-ring did not flow far enough up to the senior officials responsible for delaying the launch. Later testimony from these engineers and managers found that they had done tests, studies and improvements that led them to believe the O-ring would not cause a crash; still, they should have communicated the risk to the appropriate decision-makers in the upper organizational rungs at NASA. Instead, they kept the O-ring problem to themselves, and many lives were lost.

An organization with many "undiscussables " is an organization with low trust. The leader's interpersonal skills, along with the culture created by those skills, heavily impact that situation. Ask yourself the following questions regarding trust in your organization:

- Do you "shoot" the messenger who delivers bad news, or do you reward that person for bringing it to your attention?

- Is "good team player" a euphemism in your organization for someone who knows when to keep his mouth shut, or is there a lively discussion by all with many questions asked?

- Is "group think" alive and well in your organization, or do you praise and reward those who offer alternate views?

- After an important meeting, is the water cooler talk consistent with what was said in the meeting, or do people share their "real feelings" there?

DO NOT LET YOUR OPINION BECOME THE TRUTH

Connected leaders tend to ask more questions and make fewer statements than those who have not developed interpersonal skills. Leaders *should* have opinions, but the leader's opinion should not be the only one that counts. No leader has all the answers.

A helpful way to think about stating your position is to do it somewhat tentatively. Your opinion is just that: your opinion. It is not the whole truth. People who are effective at interpersonal skills are willing to have their assumptions disconfirmed in service to a higher goal. Colin Powell, former secretary of state and career soldier, has been quoted as saying, "Avoid having your ego so close to your position that when your position falls, your ego goes with it." Good interpersonal skills are not about protecting your ego or position; they are about getting more brains in the game through skillful conversation, minimizing undiscussables and getting as much meaning out in the open as possible. A leader who changes his discourse from "This is the way it is" to "This is the way I am thinking about it. What am I missing?" is improving his interpersonal skills. Ask yourself, "Do I advocate my position so strongly that others clam up?" and "Do I keep my opinion to myself so others have to guess what I am thinking?"

There is an old quote by Dr. W. Edwards Deming, a leading personality in the quality revolution, that says, "In God we trust. All others bring data." In tomorrow's organizations, data trumps hierarchy, and leaders should seek information from their teams.

STAY UNDER CONTROL

Paradoxically, having good interpersonal skills starts with having good intrapersonal skills, or self-awareness and self-regulation. When your ego is under control, when you are feeling comfortable with yourself and not fearful, is when it is easiest to practice good interpersonal skills. The limits of these talents are tested when "buttons get pushed" and emotions take over a conversation. When this happens, it can be easy to say things you immediately wish you could take back; such impulsive statements break the interpersonal connection.

Effective leaders are emotionally passionate about their vision but are not easily angered by another person's words or actions. To work on this piece of your interpersonal skills, you need to mentally be both "on the field and in the press box" so you can be aware of and observe situations when you are frustrated or your emotions take over. Be your own coach. Notice what brings the negative emotions on. Take ownership of your emotions. Realize that your anger belongs to you. Someone else cannot make you angry—you choose to react with anger. If you are struggling in this area, you might discuss it with a friend or advisor. Ask yourself, "How else can I better respond to this situation?" If you often "lose it" under certain conditions, diagnose why. Then, use these observations next time a frustrating situation occurs as a practice field to improve your interpersonal skills.

Emotional intelligence researchers tell us that the chemicals released by the body when emotions rise—the ones that set off the fight or flight response—can stay in the body for several hours. A one-minute outburst will affect you much longer than one minute. Although you may think you have moved past the angry response, your body thinks otherwise. Negative emotions will color your behavior for some time.

You cannot be an effective leader when negative emotions are driving your behavior. Your interpersonal skills will probably drop precipitously during this time. As you work through the various emotional situations in your life and gradually get better at dealing with them, you can limit those negative chemicals and be more effective more of the time.

As you review your emotional situations, remember that you can always choose how you respond. When someone or something upsets you, remember that it was you, not the other person, who created those feelings in yourself. If you are not happy with your reaction, ask yourself a few questions. You may need the help of a trusted advisor or coach as you work through them:

1. What was my emotional outburst really about?

2. Was there something I was afraid I might lose?

3. What assumptions did I make?

4. What meaning did I add to the actual situation? Be sure to separate the facts and data from the story in your brain.

5. How much did my history with this person color my response?

6. Does this sequence of events and emotions recur with me and other people?

7. Am I responding from past experiences and opinions? If so, is that the best approach here?

8. When this situation arises again in the future, is there a better way for me to handle it?

9. What needs to change inside me for that to happen?

10. Am I willing to make that change? If not, what do I care more about than being an effective leader?

CLARIFY YOUR INTENTIONS

If you meet regularly with a group, such as at a staff meeting, and you are interested in improving your interpersonal skills, consider eliciting help. Begin by explaining to the group what you want to work on, why you want to work on it and what you will attempt to do differently. Then, ask for their help. That way, when they see a change in you at the next meeting, they will not have to guess what you are up to.

That is also the perfect place to begin talking about how the group can improve their conversations with each other. Discuss how everyone can appropriately express their emotions while remaining authentic. In other words, review the real (unspoken) ground rules of your meetings, and make sure they are supporting what you want to accomplish. Ask the group the following questions to start a discussion:

1. What values are currently affecting conversations within the group?

2. Is it acceptable to raise voices or be disrespectful to others in your meetings?

3. Is it acceptable to disagree?

4. Is it acceptable to hold each other (peers) accountable?

5. What else cannot be said or done that is preventing you from having the most effective meetings? Would it be okay to bring these issues up in a meeting and decide how to better handle them?

TAKE CARE OF YOURSELF

We mentioned in the previous "Stay Under Control" section, emotions are closely tied to our physical state. As Vince Lombardi put it, "Fatigue makes cowards of us all." Make sure you are not neglecting your body's needs, including physical, mental, social and spiritual renewal. Such neglect will have a direct effect on your interpersonal skills, as well as your long-term relationships and leadership. You are not exempt from needing to replenish your systems to keep your body functioning. As Dr. Stephen R. Covey reminds us, take time to sharpen the saw. Use these questions to do a self-audit on how well you are taking care of yourself:

• How much real exercise are you getting? Are you doing something to raise your heart rate for thirty minutes at least five times a week? If not, go for a walk or ride a bike. A thirty-minute walk will do much more for you than watching thirty minutes of television.

- Do you have some interests or hobbies outside of work? If not, try to build a life outside of the workplace.

- Do you have a circle of people you care about and who care about you? Do you talk with them regularly? If not, or if you would like to strengthen this part of your life, schedule a few phone calls or a non-business luncheon with a friend or family member next week. If you are physically away from them, use social media to keep in touch.

- Do you have a regular spiritual practice such as meditation, prayer or reading spiritual works? If not, consider starting one or more of these with a small group of friends for mutual support and structure.

JOIN AN ORGANIZATION

Joining a service or business organization may help you become more comfortable developing business relationships. As we mentioned in "3.3 Presenting Skills," one organization that has helped many leaders become better interpersonal communicators is Toastmasters (www.toastmasters.org). The organization has chapters nearly everywhere and is a great way to improve interpersonal skills. Joining a service club such as Rotary is also a great option. Think of joining and being active as an investment in your own development and a way to enhance your perspective on the world.

GET FEEDBACK

To quote author and coach Tim Gallwey, "Awareness is curative." Working with a coach who can assess your normal behavioral preferences and natural talents will help develop awareness and other skills. Regardless of your intent, you may be impacting others in a less than positive way. Once you realize your impact, you can choose more effective behaviors and consciously implement them until they become a natural part of who you are.

Another way to get feedback is through assessments that focus on behavioral style, interpersonal skills and emotional intelligence. A number of valid instruments are available, ranging from self-tests to 360-degree feedback. For more on the tools we use with clients, contact us at support@TheCompleteLeader.org.

Your interpersonal skills will not improve unless your behavior improves. Getting feedback is like stepping on a scale: you may be more aware of your weight, but you have not lost any. Evaluate your feedback. Then, create and implement a series of behavioral experiments to improve. Continue to evaluate. See if your experiments produce their desired results. This is another place where using the Plan-Do-Check-Act process is helpful in your personal and professional life (see "Plan-Do-Check-Act" under "1.3 Planning and Organization" for more on this process).

PERSUASION

WHAT IS PERSUASION?

Think about Martin Luther King Jr.'s "I have a dream" or President Kennedy's "We will put a man on the moon" speech. Reflect on the most successful coaches, ministers and politicians. The one thing they have in common is the ability to persuade through their communication. They appeal to logic, reason, habits, emotions, desires and, sometimes, personal power to achieve their desired ends.

Persuasion is the ability to convince others to change their actions, decisions, opinions or thinking. It is influence through communication. When we refer to persuasion, we mean ethical persuasion. Although Hitler and Jim Jones were persuasive, that is not the kind of persuasion we are advocating.

Persuasive people are generally friendly, polite, trustworthy and knowledgeable. People are not persuaded by someone they do not trust or believe. Persuasive people communicate well verbally, listen to and understand the needs of others, and are able to present ideas from another's point of view. They can adapt their comments to be effective with different audiences without being duplicitous or pandering. Such individuals present ideas in a logical and reasonable manner and combine their logic with a positive emotional appeal. They see others as allies and collaborators, not adversaries. Persuasion at its best can inspire people to make commitments and achieve results they did not think possible.

> "You cannot reason people out of a position that they did not reason themselves into."
>
> – Ben Goldacre

People who have not yet developed the skills of persuasion may believe only their points of view matter. They are not adept at reading nonverbal language or presenting ideas in an appealing way. If this describes you, there are ways to improve persuasiveness.

WHY IS PERSUASION IMPORTANT?

Persuasion is the way leaders become leaders. Without influence, there is no leadership. There may be positional power, or coercion, but not true leadership. Why? Because great leaders have followers who *choose* to follow them. Followers are not slaves. They are humans who have free will and the power of choice. The decision of whether to follow depends on how well the leader persuades. Effective leaders inspire others to make commitments they might not otherwise make.

HOW IS PERSUASION LEARNED?

As you develop your basic talents for listening, diplomacy, speaking respectfully and other interpersonal skills, you will also be reinforcing what it takes to persuade others. Persuasion can be learned. The following tips will get you started.

SELF-EVALUATE

What is your preferred style for persuading others? Do you favor a hard approach based on positional power or some other outside commodity? These methods of persuasion are usually based on threats and fear, like the parent who says, "If you don't clean up your room, I am going to ground you until you are 35." Perhaps you prefer a soft approach, such as, "You didn't clean up your room like I asked, so I will do it for you." That is emotional manipulation or management by guilt.

> ## "If you want more, you need to be more."
> ## – Jim Rohn

There is a better approach than either of those. The "better approach" is usually based on reliability and mutual trust. As we mentioned, people must choose to let you influence them. Yes, you can persuade someone with a threat or guilt, but that is not persuasion—and it is not great leadership. It is coercion. And it only works until the person you are trying to persuade can get away from your threat.

OBSERVE HOW OTHERS PERSUADE

As you are examining your own persuasion style, also be aware of how others influence you. What are they doing that you like? What do you not like? Why? Do you remember a time when someone got you to do something, even though you thought you could not do it? Could you "borrow" some of the approaches used by those you admire and who have persuaded you?

You may find that persuasive people speak in the language of those whom they want to influence. They make it easy for potential followers to understand their message. The message usually resonates with the intended audience because they combine emotion and logic so the message is received in several parts of the brain.

Next time you get a chance, watch great speakers. Their messages are often wrapped in stories, usually first-person accounts that move the audience. Narratives, especially emotional ones, are powerful methods of persuasion because people relate to them. Compelling speakers usually tell stories in common, everyday language and include emotional components as well as factual ones.

BE CREDIBLE, RATIONAL AND PASSIONATE

To be persuasive, you must first be credible. Your audience starts with a bias toward you that greatly affects your ability to persuade. If they are meeting you for the first time, their biases are based largely on first impressions. If they already know you, your credibility is made up of their past experiences with you, for better or worse. This means they will start pulling the lever to vote for or against you before you even open your mouth. A poor reputation is not impossible to overcome, but consider whether you need to work on strengthening your reputation as the foundation or precursor to persuasion. To help build credibility, you may want to review "3.3 Presenting Skills," specifically the sections on authenticity and eliminating sloppy speech, movements and appearance.

> "To be persuasive we must be believable; to be believable we must be credible; to be credible we must be truthful."
> – Edward R. Murrow

Next, your message must be rational. It needs to make basic sense and be understandable. One of the main reasons people fail to persuade others is that their message is too confusing and complex. Make your message simple enough that you can explain it to an eighth grader, in a way that he can then describe it to another adult.

Finally, your words need the passion of conviction and commitment behind them. As Zig Ziglar said, "The first sale begins with you!" Make sure you are passionate about your topic, and let that show through as you persuade.

HAVE A PLAN

If you want to persuade others to your way of thinking and acting, create a presentation plan ahead of time. The plan needs to be logical and reasonable in the eyes of your audience and stir positive emotion within them. People want to be "moved," not just convinced. Your message needs to include both what you want them to do and why they should do it. Individuals want to know, "What's in it for me?" Show them why your idea is an effective and rewarding use of their time and energy.

> "Think twice before you speak, because your words and influence will plant the seed of either success or failure in the mind of another."
>
> – Napoleon Hill

As a part of your plan, create a short summary statement of what you want to accomplish. Make it your goal to explain your point of view in thirty seconds or less. You might even think of a clever short saying or aphorism to capture the main kernel of your idea; make sure it is simple enough so that people "get it" quickly. President Kennedy said, "I believe that this nation should commit itself to achieving the goal, before this decade is out, of landing a man on the moon and returning him safely to the earth." This simple sentence stirred emotion and pride in the United States, and was a catalyst to the space program that followed.

EXPECT RESISTANCE

Be prepared for resistance to your idea, and do not be put off by it. See it as the way some people consider your message before buying in. Acknowledge their points of view by restating them to their satisfaction, and then politely explain how your view both agrees with and differs from their approaches. Help them overcome their resistance. Remember, the people you want to persuade are, or will be, your allies. Treat them as such from the beginning. Do not set up adversarial relationships.

DO NOT GO FOR THE QUICK FIX

When working on your persuasion style, beware of people who suggest "secret ways" to influence others. This is called manipulation and includes anything done to others that is not in their best interests. These techniques will lose power if those you are attempting to influence discover your "trick." Manipulation is the opposite of being open, authentic and honest. Stay away from these methods because they will not serve you well in the long term.

> **"Don't raise your voice, improve your argument."**
> **– Desmond Tutu**

BE THE CHANGE

If you want to have genuine influence with others, be open to their influence on you. As Gandhi put it, "If we could change ourselves, the tendencies in the world would also change. As a man changes his own nature, so does the attitude of the world change towards him."

While listening to others, do you search for what might open up a new possibility, or do you listen to them as a judge and critic, to find the flaw in their reasoning? Even if you do not particularly like a person, try to listen, remembering that everyone deserves courtesy and respect. Listen as the beginner, not the expert. People who listen as experts already "know" and are usually not open to influence. Beginners are open to many possibilities.

Grow to be the expert by always remaining open to others' ideas. Be a lifelong learner by listening to people and their experiences. You will not live long enough to make all the mistakes you need to make to become the expert in everything. Profit from others' knowledge, as well as your own. And remember to be the change you seek in others.

NEGOTIATION

WHAT IS NEGOTIATION?

Randy was listening in as customer service representatives at a utility company took phone calls from residential users. These reps spent their days on the telephone dealing with customers. Most of the customers they talked to had some kind of problem—an issue with their bill or pending disconnection due to an unpaid balance, for example.

In a job like that, which constantly deals with problems, it can be easy for the reps to become jaded and believe that all callers are trying to beat the system. Conversely, reps can develop a soft heart and believe that all of the callers are having a run of bad luck, and that the rep should do whatever she can to help relieve the problem. But applying these general beliefs is not accurate for all callers, of course. If a rep were to listen to the customers out of either a jaded or soft paradigm, she would not be listening objectively. Therefore, she would not be able to solve problems in the best manner.

The best of these call center representatives assumed nothing. They followed a process for gathering information that allowed them to clearly understand the problem from the caller's perspective and used appropriate empathy to relate with the emotions of the customer. Randy could hear customers calm down as the reps restated the problems to the callers' satisfaction. The customers could tell the reps were listening, and the callers' anger dissipated.

At that point, the reps would move to problem-solving and negotiating and make suggestions for how the issue might be solved for the customer, keeping in mind both what the customer wanted and what the utility company needed. The reps often came up with an alternative that worked for both the customers and the company and dealt with each customer in a factual, unemotional manner. Although there was often some back and forth discussion, the reps stayed objective. Most of the customers ended up thanking the reps, even if they did not get exactly what they wanted. This is the essence of effective negotiation.

Negotiation is a conversation that constructively facilitates an agreement between two or more people. People who excel at negotiation consider all opinions and facts before drawing conclusions. They start out "dumb," meaning that they do not assume anything about the negotiation. Good negotiators definitely do not assume conflict, which allows them to listen objectively to all parties. When difficult issues arise, they face them objectively and negotiate acceptable solutions by creating and exploring common expectations and mutual benefits.

Leaders who are not skilled in negotiation react in one of two ways. One way is to ignore issues and conflicts and not deal with them. These people say things like, "Don't bring me bad news," or "Deal with that yourself." In effect, they abdicate their responsibility for dealing with what they consider to be messy stuff. Of course, leaders are not responsible for settling everyone's issues. But leaders need to do what is necessary to keep people working well together in service to the mission. This may include teaching team members how to deal with their own issues, which increases each individual's capacity for productive negotiations.

The second reaction of leaders who are not skilled in negotiation is to overreact. They jump into the middle of a conflict and unilaterally resolve it. These leaders are insensitive to others' need to be heard. Such resolutions are often short-lived because the people involved did not feel heard or understood; instead of abiding by the leader's resolution, they will find some other path to attempt to get what they want. The leader may think he "saved time," but his quick solution usually takes more time in the long run because the decision comes unraveled. Also, his intervention does nothing to improve the capabilities of the followers to negotiate their own issues in the future. In fact, the followers will become less adept at resolving issues if they believe they can run to the leader for a solution!

WHY IS NEGOTIATION IMPORTANT?

As shown by the customer service representatives in the previous story, effective negotiation builds the reputation of a company. In every organization, employees are "negotiating" every day with their customers. These interactions, over time, can make or break a company.

Similarly, negotiation is critical to maintaining unity within an organization. In the future, people will become even more interconnected and interdependent with others around the globe. Any complex project will involve a diverse set of interested parties, each with their own wants and needs. The ability to negotiate innovative solutions that include all parties will be a critical asset for tomorrow's leaders.

Negotiation skills support a leader's ability to manage differences and bring disparate parties together to achieve a goal. Leaders rarely find the paths to their visions straight and clear. On their journeys, they need help from others—people who also have their own agendas and desires. A leader who can use his skills of listening and asking questions to learn what the other party wants, while being open enough to share his own interests, will be able to build a foundation for a positive negotiation and success.

HOW IS NEGOTIATION LEARNED?

CHOOSE TO BE A WIN-WIN NEGOTIATOR

The place to begin learning negotiation is inside your own head. Be clear about your intention. Make sure you are not looking for a slick way to get what you want while not caring about the people you are negotiating with. This shortsighted approach will only work if you are not planning on doing business with those people ever again. Even in that case, your reputation as a bad-faith negotiator will spread and limit your power and influence.

> "Everything is negotiable. Whether or not the negotiation is easy is another thing."
> – Carrie Fisher

Consider yourself and the other parties as parts of a larger whole. Therefore, harming others equals harming yourself. Negotiating does not need to be a win-lose contest. When your intention is to treat the other party as a partner, and to jointly try to find a mutually beneficial solution, then, and only then, are you ready to learn the skills of modern negotiation. If any party feels unfairly treated, a negotiation cannot be considered a success.

In 1980, George Mitchell became a U.S. Senator and quickly earned a reputation as a skilled negotiator. In a 2012 CBS News interview, Mitchell said he would ask himself, "Why do they believe as they do? Why do they act as they do? Is there something to their position that I don't understand or that I've been wrong about? The most disturbing thing now is the rigidity of some—you know, 'We are right, we are 100 percent right, and if you disagree with us, you're not just wrong, you're not an American.'" Any leader would do well to follow his example.

UNDERSTAND THE BASICS

There are many courses available on negotiation, although some still advocate the shortsighted "get as much as you can" approach. Check for courses online, or at your local college or university, or visit our website at www.TheCompleteLeader.org for more on developing the skill of negotiation.

One way to begin cultivating a firm foundation is by reading. There are many books available about negotiation, and there are sure to be many more written. Two classics include Gerard Nierenberg's *The Art of Negotiating* and Roger Fisher's and William Ury's *Getting to Yes*. Fisher and Ury advocate four basic steps to principled negotiating:

1. **Separate the people from the problem.** It is important to not let relational tensions overwhelm the negotiating process. When they do, negotiations become ego contests, where one person usually wins at the expense of the other. (For more on this, see "Be Soft on the People and Hard on the Problem" later in this module.)

2. **Focus on interests, not positions.** When negotiators make ultimatums and arbitrary statements (i.e. taking positions), negotiating denigrates into misunderstandings and accu-

sations of greed, self-centeredness and stubbornness. (See "Choose Shared Interest Over Self-Interest" later in this module.)

3. **Generate a variety of possibilities before deciding what to do.** Instead of just choosing one solution and moving forward with implementation, focus on building a creative list of possible solutions. Brainstorming a big list of possibilities prepares all parties in a negotiation to listen and consider ideas, no matter who the author is.

4. **Insist that the result be based on some objective standard.** When a negotiated outcome is based on an objective standard, there is no question whether or not the outcome has been reached.

LEARN FROM EXPERIENCE

Negotiation is one talent that you can improve by learning from experience. Every time you work with someone to make a decision, it is an opportunity to develop your skills. Notice what both you and others do that is effective and ineffective during negotiation, and incorporate what you like into your own negotiating style.

> *"You can only end a negotiation for peace if you begin it."*
>
> – Benjamin Netanyahu

CHOOSE SHARED INTEREST OVER SELF-INTEREST

Understanding the difference between a "position" and an "interest," and how to move from one to the other, is key to principled negotiations. A position is a statement of what someone wants. Let us say a couple, Kyle and Sarah, both have different ideas of what they want to do for dinner. Kyle says, "I want to go to Tasteless Bar-B-Que for dinner," while Sarah says, "I want to eat at home."

When these two wants are expressed, one of several scenarios can result: an argument, a power struggle, or a civilized negotiation and problem-solving session.

If the couple continues to talk at the level of their positions, there is not much wiggle room for a solution. Dinner will either be at the restaurant or at home, and someone will win and someone will lose. If a win-lose pattern repeats itself often enough in a relationship, the relationship will degrade to lose-lose, as the person on the short end decides enough is enough. Win-lose and lose-win are both temporary situations, and both will eventually become lose-lose. The only long-term, sustainable approach is win-win. That requires each party to look out not only for their own win, but also the win of the others involved.

Luckily, this couple does not need to go down the lose-lose path. They can be patient and take the time to listen to each other to understand the "why" of their positions. In other words, they can give up their *positions* and can explore their *interests*—what they are each interested in getting or doing that led each one to their positions. It might go something like this:

> "Okay, hold on. Before we get into another argument about where to eat, tell me why you want to eat at home," Kyle says.

> "I have been on the go all day," Sarah responds. "I just got here. I'm really beat, and I'd like to just fix a sandwich, have a glass of wine and watch the news. Why do you want to go to Tasteless?"

> "I don't know, exactly. I've just got a craving for some good barbeque and a beer."

> "Yeah, barbeque sounds pretty good to me, too, but I honestly have no energy for going out."

"I can understand that. Well, what can we do to get what we both want?" Kyle reasons.

We will interrupt this dialogue here to let you offer your own advice. Can you think of three or four scenarios that would get them what they both want? Of course you can.

Two positions can appear, at the beginning, to be opposed to each other. But, remember, these positions are just one of many strategies for people to get what they want. Moving from self-interest to shared interest is the key move of successful negotiators. This mind-set is built on being considerate of the needs of others, while being courageous enough to ask for what you need.

The point is: When you begin a negotiation, your position is only one of several possible solutions for you to get what you want. It is probably the one you thought of first, and it is easy to quit thinking about other solutions. A better approach is to get over the habit of insisting on your first solution; expand the conversation to explore options to include the other party's wants. Then, find a resolution that achieves most or all of what you both want. Using this approach, you can become a skilled negotiator.

A mistake made by many negotiators is moving to the solution part of the negotiation too quickly by creating an action plan before taking the time to fully explore the interests of all parties. Once you take the time to discover shared interests, they create the foundation for an innovative solution that all parties will buy into. If you keep track of these win-win negotiations over time, you will also find that taking time to discover the interests of all involved will actually save time in the long run. The final solution will be more acceptable to everyone and will have less chance of coming unraveled in the future.

BE SOFT ON THE PEOPLE AND HARD ON THE PROBLEM

In *Getting to Yes*, Fisher and Ury also offer good advice: be hard on the problem, soft on the people. Being hard on the problem means taking time to collect all the facts and data relevant to the negotiations, including clear definitions of what acceptable outcomes might look like.

> **"During a negotiation, it would be wise not to take anything personally. If you leave personalities out of it, you will be able to see opportunities more objectively."**
>
> **– Brian Koslow**

The CBS News interview with George Mitchell revealed that, on the first day after he was elected Democratic Senate Majority Leader in 1989, Mitchell made a pledge to Republican Leader Bob Dole. He said, "I'll never try to embarrass you. I will never attack you personally." Surely that respectful approach to others was a key to his success and a great example of being "soft on the people."

Dole said, "It's almost unheard of these days, but in those days, it was a cordiality. We had a relationship. He's my friend and he's a great legislator."

KEEP "NO DEAL" AS AN OPTION

Not all negotiations reach a mutual agreement. It is a measure of integrity to know when to walk away—and to actually do it. Dr. Stephen R. Covey's advice is "think win-win or no deal." Covey says it is better to walk away from an agreement that you do not feel good about, and to salvage the relationship as best you can, than to make a lose-win or a win-lose deal. Perhaps you will find yourself in a better negotiation with this person in the future.

CONSIDER USING A THIRD PARTY

Sometimes, neutral third parties can handle negotiations more effectively than the people or groups involved. The third-party mediator may meet with the various sides separately to explore their interests and remove some of the emotional noise that often occurs when all parties are in the room together. Ron helped a client negotiate through a third-party mediator recently, and the result was a savings of $1 million, from just one day of focused efforts by all parties involved. Politicians refer to this method as "shuttle diplomacy." Professional athletes normally delegate negotiating to their agents. Do not limit your options or venues. Instead, match your approach to the realities, possibilities and circumstances surrounding the issues at hand.

3.9

CONFLICT MANAGEMENT

WHAT IS CONFLICT MANAGEMENT?

While not every negotiation involves conflict, some clearly do. Conflict can be found in families, organizations, cities and countries. A conflict occurs when two or more parties disagree or want contradictory outcomes. Conflicts are often characterized by high emotion and low trust, which makes the conflict management conversation particularly difficult.

Disagreements are often created when people represent different parts of a system. For instance, the person from Finance wants to keep costs down, but the project manager wants to use a vendor who provides higher-quality parts and is a bit more expensive. This can quickly devolve into conflict, based on different corporate goals. Notice that this situation may feel personal but comes from the positions represented and not necessarily from the individuals in those positions.

Conflict can also result from different values. One team member wants to take time to collect more data on a problem; another wants to move ahead for fear of missing a deadline. Although this type of conflict may be considered more "personal" since it is based on intrinsic motivators, or what a person believes is important, it is not personal in the sense that one team member wants to irritate the other (see "Discover Your Intrinsic Motivation" under "Part Two: Leaders Lead Themselves" for more on motivators). It is more about one person wanting to do what he values as significant.

> "The quality of our lives depends not on whether or not we have conflicts, but on how we respond to them."
>
> – Tom Crum

WHY IS CONFLICT MANAGEMENT IMPORTANT?

As we mentioned in "3.8 Negotiation," any complex project involves a diverse set of interested parties, each with their own motivations, wants and needs. The ability to negotiate innovative solutions that consider all involved will be an increasingly critical asset for tomorrow's leaders. Effective conflict negotiators can "put out the fire" of high emotions and even build confidence in a low-trust environment. These leaders keep teams cohesive and working toward a solution that serves everyone.

As the world constantly shifts boundaries, today's opponent may be tomorrow's partner. This means that if you make another person a "loser" today by zero-sum negotiation, it will be much harder to recruit that person as an ally tomorrow. Interdependence means your "win" is inescapably tied to the other party's "win," and conflict management skills will improve your odds of creating a win-win outcome.

HOW IS CONFLICT MANAGEMENT LEARNED?

People skilled in conflict management are competent practitioners of the principled negotiation approach we discussed in "3.8

Negotiation." Principled negotiating seeks to find mutual agreements that balance results with relationships. If you want to improve your conflict negotiation skills, start there. Then, consider the following:

DEAL WITH EMOTIONS BEFORE FACTS

If emotions are so high that civil discourse is impossible, suggest a cooling-off period. When you reconvene, be willing to listen to the other party to understand the conflict from his point of view, without being defensive or critical. Refer to "How Is Empathy Learned?" in "3.1 Empathy" to help you.

Ask yourself, "Why does the other person see the situation differently?" and, if applicable, "Why does he feel threatened?" You may discover that he is afraid of some kind of loss. He may fear losing something good or getting something that he does not want if he agrees to your idea.

> **"In conflict, be fair and generous."**
>
> **– Lao Tzu**

Be diligent in managing the conflict. Keep talking and listening until you can state the other person's position better than he can. People are more willing to work on solving a problem when they feel understood.

BUILD RESPECT AND TRUST

See the other person as a reasonable, rational, decent human being. Listening to understand builds respect and trust. You can respect a person without agreeing with her, or even liking her. Every person deserves a level of respect, just for being human.

Acknowledge past differences or grievances, if appropriate, and then keep the conversation centered on the present and near future. Work with what is happening *now*, not what has occurred in the past. Be willing to state what you need, as well as what you understand the other party needs—do not make them guess.

> ## "Never cut what you can untie."
> ## – Joseph Joubert

Also, work to build trust. If complete confidence isn't warranted, you can give conditional trust. See the other party more as a collaborator than a competitor. Even more importantly, be trustworthy. Make promises sparingly and keep them. Do what you say you are going to do. In the end, that is the best way to build trust with another person.

SEE CONFLICT AS A POSITIVE

Conflict does not need to remain a negative. If handled well, conflict can improve relationships, get "undiscussable" topics out in the open, provide a more complete picture of a situation, reduce delays and other tactics that get in the way of project completion, reduce stress, and raise the trust level in an organization. Focus on the positive aspects of conflict as an incentive to deal with it quickly and effectively.

Conversely, avoiding conflict will not resolve it. In fact, doing so usually results in more conflict later, and the issue will be on your mind until you deal with it. Shawn Kent Hayashi, an executive coach and colleague of ours, recommends that if you think about something troubling three or more times, challenge yourself to address it and take steps for achieving resolution.

Alfred P. Sloan, who was key in building General Motors, saw the positive side of ideological conflict and understood it so deeply that he incorporated it into his management decision-making process. Sloan was known to delay making important decisions until he and his senior leaders had thoroughly debated all options. Instead of avoiding this type of conflict, he demanded that these debates include rigor (well-researched data) and vigor (passionate arguments). He had several reasons for taking this approach to dealing with ideological conflict. He wanted:

- **Leaders to think critically and deeply about important decisions.** He did not want them surrendering to a superficial consensus that seemed obvious at the moment but prove shortsighted or inadequate in the future.

- **The team to think creatively.** He encouraged individuals to open their minds to many possibilities and collect an abundance of ideas. After they had done that, they could sort through the options to determine which were best.

- **Several options developed.** Sloan realized that a great decision today could become a bad decision in six months for reasons beyond anyone's control. By developing several options at some depth, he would have well-vetted contingencies already created if future circumstances changed. All he had to do was take them off the shelf for implementation.

- **Rigorous and vigorous debate.** He believed in "group wisdom," not to be confused by "groupthink." Sloan held that intelligent minds were sharpened and better ideas were germinated in the laboratories of vigorous debate.

Ron will often challenge the leadership teams he works with to follow Sloan's example. To practice, they first establish the ground rules for debate. Then, they come up with some fictional topics to assess and dispute, learning to argue for or against an issue based on the flip of a coin. When Ron is convinced they are engaged and becoming skillful, they move to "practicing" with real issues currently being faced by their organization. In both of these activities, the emphasis is not on the issues or who is winning; the focus is on developing broader and deeper skills, both in logic and expression of ideas. After the team members have proven some mastery in managing this ideological conflict, Ron moves them into addressing their most critical issues and making weighty decisions. You may want to try this approach with your team.

> **"Peace is not the absence of conflict, but the presence of creative alternatives for responding to conflict..."**
> **– Dorothy Thompson**

Ron's friend Jim Stephens refers to conflict as the "doorway to intimacy." When conflict is managed effectively, it can bring new levels of understanding, empathy and trust between parties. When conflict leads to this type of collaboration and new alternatives that improve on the original idea, it seems almost magic. For more on how to create the magic, visit our website at www.TheCompleteLeader.org.

3.10

TEAMWORK

WHAT IS TEAMWORK?

Every other year since 1927, top golfers in the U.S. and Europe form teams to compete in the Ryder Cup. Professional golfers who spend most of their careers competing as individuals spend one week together as a team to uphold the honor and tradition of their respective teams. Though the United States consistently boasts the highest individual rankings in the world among their team members, the European team has dominated the competition in the twenty-first century (five wins to one at the time of publication). How can this happen? Most commentators speculate that though the United States claims the best individual talent in the world, the Europeans know something more about competing as a team.

Teamwork is a group of individuals working together to achieve a common objective. A person with a talent for teamwork enjoys working cooperatively with others to achieve group goals. This type of person supports team members, does not second-guess team decisions and contributes positively to team projects.

People who lack a talent for teamwork prefer to work individually and independently. They do not want to be held responsible for contributing to a larger team goal or picking up the slack for a team member who is not pulling his weight. They are more focused on self-interest than shared interest.

WHY IS TEAMWORK IMPORTANT?

In the past, information flowed down and work flowed up. The hierarchical structure of most organizations supported a vertically focused group of specialists who worked in "silos." Employees worked for their boss, who worked for his boss. Little information or resources flowed "horizontally" in an organization.

> "Teamwork is so important that it is virtually impossible for you to reach the heights of your capabilities or make the money that you want without becoming very good at it."
> – Brian Tracy

Increasingly, information and other resources must flow in *all* directions. Transparency will be one of the new currencies. The need for resources to be available far beyond artificial department and division boundaries will be paramount to success. Supply chains and logistics chains are present-day examples of this horizontal movement. In these environments, teams form to complete a project, then disband, only to reform with different members for the next project.

Teamwork is also important because leadership is not an individual sport. Independence has been replaced by interdependence—and it will be even more so in the future. The essence of leadership is accomplishing worthy goals through the combined efforts of others, realizing that everyone's goal is to serve the mission and the customers, not the boss.

The important projects of the future will often span geographies, time zones and cultures, and involve more than one organization. Teams may be "virtual" and even located in different parts of the world. As we have noted, the ability to cooperate and move beyond self-interest to shared interest and common ground are hallmarks of an effective workforce. A talent for teamwork is a necessity.

HOW IS TEAMWORK LEARNED?

START WITH THE TEAM CLOSEST TO YOU

The best place to create an effective team is with the people you work directly with. To understand the significance of this, we must distinguish the difference between a team and a work group. A work group is one or more people who do similar work, possibly in the same geographical location, but are not interdependent or necessarily committed to a group goal. A team is a group of people who work together in order to achieve a group goal.

> "Individual commitment to a group effort—that is what makes a team work, a company work, a society work, a civilization work."
> – Vince Lombardi, legendary football coach of the Green Bay Packers

Napoleon Hill included an interview with Andrew Carnegie, founder of Carnegie Steel Company, in his book *Think and Grow Rich* that emphasizes this point. In the interview, Carnegie explained how he had assembled a "mastermind group" of about fifty people who worked for him. Carnegie said he did not know what all it took to manufacture and deliver steel, but the men in the mastermind group knew everything about that subject. Carnegie said his job as CEO was not to know all the details about making steel; his job was to keep the mastermind group functioning effectively. As a manager, are you making sure keeping your direct reports functioning effectively as a team is a key part of your job?

ASSESS YOUR PRESENT TEAM

Here are a few questions to help you get a quick idea of the effectiveness of your present team:

- Is your team integrated and committed to each other, or are people on your team just there to protect their own interests?

- How are decisions made? Are they discussed, or does the leader provide most of the answers?

- Does the team use everyone's thinking or just that of the vocal minority?

- Are roles, goals and measures of success clearly defined for each person?

- Is "team member" a designated part of the job for each individual on your team?

- Does your team take the time to critique their own meetings and make process improvements?

- Are commitments met? If not, is there a diagnosis of what went wrong in the process? How do team members hold each other accountable for work and results?

- Do your team members put up with mediocrity? Do you?

If you are not satisfied with the answers to any of these questions, discuss your concerns in an upcoming meeting. See if the team agrees with you, and try to work out the issue.

KNOW THE FOUR STAGES OF TEAM GROWTH

In 1965, Bruce Tuckman identified four phases of team development: forming, storming, norming and performing. Determine what phase your team is in and what you can do to move it to the next phase. With skilled leadership, teams can get through the forming and storming stages quicker, and get on to the norming and performing stages, which are about creating results. For more information on these four phases of team growth, visit www.TheCompleteLeader.org.

PRACTICE GOOD TEAM MEMBER BEHAVIORS

Almost everyone in an organization is a member of at least one team. That includes you, even if you do not consider your group a "team." By modeling good behaviors yourself, you might encourage others to raise the effectiveness of the teams you are on. At the least, you will be welcomed as a productive and cooperative team member. Good team member behaviors are common sense for anyone who works with others—which includes almost everyone. The following are ways you can exhibit good team member behaviors:

- **Prioritize**: Make being a team member a priority and not an intrusion into your "real" job.

- **Communicate**: Be an active part of all discussions, even those that are not in your area of expertise. Ask questions. Contribute ideas. Summarize and pull various ideas together. Encourage and support other team members, and disagree when appropriate.

- **Take action**: Complete any work assigned to you. Support others when they need help, while helping them remain accountable for their part of the team. Stay on task and help others do the same.

IDENTIFY THE DYSFUNCTIONS IN YOUR TEAM

A well-known resource on teamwork is *The Five Dysfunctions of a Team* by Patrick Lencioni. In it, he lists the following five "dysfunctions" for teams:

1. Absence of trust for the good intentions of others on the team; this shows up as invulnerability.

2. Fear of conflict; this shows up as artificial harmony.

3. Lack of commitment based on clarity and buy-in; this shows up as ambiguity.

4. Avoidance of peer accountability; this shows up as low standards.

5. Inattention to collective results; this shows up as status and ego.

You can easily have a conversation in one of your group meetings about how each of the above five shows up on your team, with the goal of improving teamwork.

Other practical resources can also help you learn about improving your team's effectiveness. We personally like *The Team Handbook*, which is a simple and practical guide that can be used to get things done and analyze when the group is off track.

> "A group of leaders without a common goal is not a team; it is a gathering."
>
> – Ron Price

LEARN FROM EXPERIENCE

When building a team or serving as a team member, it is important to consider three domains: relationships, results and process. All three need to work well to have a successful outcome. Ideally, a team will come together as relative strangers, learn to trust and depend on each other (relationships), while completing specific goals (results). They will meet the agreed-to metrics such as time frame, quality and cost, and they will do it using a process that is understandable, replicable and can be improved as needed.

Whether you are the team leader, a team member or an advisor, be a good ethnographer. Watch for relationships, results and process. See how one affects the other. Keep a journal of your observations. If the team shows signs of getting off track or stuck in the "storming" phase, diagnose if it is a relationships, process or results problem. Discuss the issue with the team, and help the team make midcourse corrections as needed.

EMPLOYEE DEVELOPMENT AND COACHING

WHAT ARE EMPLOYEE DEVELOPMENT AND COACHING?

Early in Randy's career, an executive several levels above Randy went out of his way to be helpful. Randy remembers that the executive was always willing to review Randy's presentations before they were taken "up the line" for corporate approval. They worked through the presentations together, and the executive suggested improvements in a way that did not belittle Randy. He also always offered to go over a presentation again after Randy made changes. This type of development and coaching demonstrates a sincere desire and ability to help improve others. Randy still remembers the experience fondly, many years later.

The word "coach" comes from the Hungarian village of Kocs (pronounced "kotch"). The village was famous for its large horse-drawn carriages, called kocsi, in the sixteenth century. In Britain, the word became coach, and by the nineteenth century, it took on the second meaning of private tutor. The implication was that the horse-drawn coach was the fastest way to get someone from where she was to her destination, much like a tutor does with learning.

Based on the word's origin, a coach is someone who helps the person being coached get to where she wants to go—to get the results she wants—in a timely manner. We believe this is still a good definition of a coach.

A person who effectively develops and coaches employees is an advocate and accountability partner for that person. The coach or mentor devotes appropriate time to the person she is working with and knows how to communicate with that person in a firm and fair way. She helps the individual being coached move toward a goal but is careful to leave the responsibility for achieving the goal with the person being coached.

A person who is not skilled at employee development and coaching does not practice this "firm and fair" coaching technique and is usually reduced to choosing either a "hard" or "soft" approach. The hard approach is sometimes called "do to" and is based on intimidation and fear. The "soft" approach, called "do for," is based on not wanting to confront or hold the other person accountable. Neither of these approaches are effective for long-term leadership.

The "do to" win-lose approach becomes lose-lose when the other person gets tired of being abused and finds a better job. The "do for" lose-win approach also results in lose-lose. Either the manager or coach gets tired of doing what the employee should be doing, or the employee gets tired of being micromanaged and not being given a chance to grow; these can result in firing or finding other employment. If you struggle with effective employee development and coaching, there are ways to foster this skill.

WHY ARE EMPLOYEE DEVELOPMENT AND COACHING IMPORTANT?

As a person develops her leadership competency, her ability to influence others grows. As she progresses in her career, her horizon broadens from department to division to organization to community to world. When she sees herself as belonging to a "larger whole," she naturally wants to improve the culture and lives of other people. One way of doing this is through employee development and coaching.

Effective leaders create more leaders. Coaching employees is a specific way to help improve an individual's ability to produce results. Can you think of a person who had a positive effect on your life? Perhaps it was someone you looked up to such as a teacher, coach, neighbor or friend. No matter what that person was called, he or she was, in effect, coaching you—helping and encouraging you to become the person you could be.

Improving the capacity and capability of those around them is the hallmark of an effective leader. This is largely done through coaching and mentoring.

> "A coach is someone who tells you what you don't want to hear, who has you see what you don't want to see, so you can be who you have always known you could be."
> – Tom Landry, former head coach
> of the Dallas Cowboys

The best leaders handle problems quickly, and coaching is an effective way to handle many types of problems because of the dual benefit of solving a problem while developing the capabilities of the person being coached. Coaching is also a fine way to start developing a new employee by overlapping the employee's needs with her obligations to the organization. Coaching helps organizations keep and develop their people because employees understand that the organization is helping them grow and contribute as individuals.

HOW ARE EMPLOYEE DEVELOPMENT AND COACHING LEARNED?

Coaching is usually focused on helping someone take advantage of an opportunity or solve a problem, meaning it is focused on a particular goal or result. The basic skills of coaching can be learned in a few days. Approaches to coaching vary, and a number of organizations offer courses and certifications to help you learn the basics. If you want to learn to coach, select an approach that is both in sync with your organization's values and suits your personality. Then, you can spend a lifetime refining and developing your own unique coaching style.

The four primary competencies of coaching are listening, creating awareness, planning and managing progress. Notice that these are also the talents necessary for leaders to get things done through others. Let us take a look at how each of these four skills enhances your ability to develop and coach employees.

LISTEN

Through the gift of listening, you demonstrate humility and respect. Additionally, new ideas often emerge when people feel free to state their thoughts out loud. When done correctly, you will work harder than the person you are coaching, because you will be listening deeply to see the problem and hear it from the coachee's point of view. For thorough discussions about listening, review "3.1 Empathy" and "3.2 Understanding and Evaluating Others."

CREATE AWARENESS

A good way to help someone become aware of her behaviors and develop a plan for improvement is to ask questions that help clarify what she wants to accomplish. Great questions create learning because they encourage thinking. As the person you are coaching answers your questions, much more learning will occur than if you were to give her a lecture. Most people, if given a safe space to "think out loud," will come up with their own plan of action. When we work with people to help them learn to coach, we use four foundational questions to raise awareness, based on the work of Dr. William Glasser and adapted for business by Ron Ernst in his book, *RealTime Coaching*. They are:

1. What do you want?

2. What are you doing? (What are you doing to get what you want?)

3. Is it working? (Self-evaluate your plan and progress.)

4. What is your plan? (What is your next step to move toward what you want?)

There are many variations on those four questions and, when used by a skillful coach with the right intention, they create awareness and help a person achieve an objective. Looking closer at these four questions, you can see that they form a closed system to help move someone (or yourself) toward a goal.

As the coachee thinks about and answers these questions, awareness surrounding what she wants and what she is doing to get it improves. Awareness creates options and actions.

The first three questions clarify wants, behaviors and results. A person becomes motivated when there is a gap between what she wants and the current results she perceives she is getting. One key to coaching is to lead the person you are working with to talk about what she wants, and then let her self-evaluate her perception of what she is getting at the time. If she sees a difference between what she wants and the results she perceives, she will very possibly come up with a better choice of behavior to close that gap. Likewise, as a coach, if you do not know her answers to the first three questions, you will not be able to help her.

As you help the person you are coaching become more aware of her present situation and how her behaviors are contributing to that situation, she often will see a new course of action open up that she did not see before. When that happens, she can create her own plan by answering the fourth question.

PLAN AND SET GOALS

A good action plan encourages people to stretch beyond what they might ordinarily think possible. The plan created at the end of each coaching conversation (the answer to, "What is your plan?") is the "feedback loop" that keeps the person being coached either moving toward, or reevaluating, the goal. Coaching without a plan is just having a conversation, with the likely outcome that the person being coached will not change what she is doing. Without an agreed-to plan, as coach, you are left to have the same conversation next time you meet.

You can also ask your coachee, "What is your next step?" or "What needs to happen next?" Sometimes, people will say something like, "I need Frank to change." If that happens, you must point out that changing may or may not be Frank's plan, but you are talking about *your* (the coachee's) plan. Ask the person you are coaching, "What do *you* need to do next?" Doing so will help return personal accountability to the person being coached.

We discussed SMART plans in "1.3 Planning and Organization" and again in "2.5 Goal Achievement." The acronym applies to creating a coaching plan, as well. Use the SMART plan questions to help the person you are coaching create an effective plan; you can also use them to create a plan for yourself. Make sure the plan is:

Specific: What one issue will you work on?

Measurable: How will we objectively know if you accomplished the plan or not?

Action-oriented: What will you *do* (stated as actions)?

Realistic: Can you realistically do what you said you would do?

Timely: When will you do it?

As a coach, when you listen to what the coachee plans to do between now and your next coaching session, make sure her plan is a SMART one.

MANAGE PROGRESS AND ACCOUNTABILITY

Done well, accountability teaches people to celebrate success, to reflect, and to correct a course when necessary. One purpose of coaching is to provide an accountability point for the person being coached. As the coach, you are not there to police and criticize when the coachee does something wrong; you are there to help her see possibilities and take action toward those possibilities. In that sense, during coaching meetings, begin by having the person look at the plan she made in the last session. Then ask, "Did you accomplish the plan you set last time?" If she says yes, then say, "Good job. What's next?" If she says no, then you say, "Okay, what is next?" In other words, see results as just results, with no judgment. Your focus is on behaviors, results and, "What are you going to do next?"

That said, do not put up with a person repeatedly missing a plan. The question then becomes, "Are you sure you want what you said you want? Because you have set a plan twice and not done it either time." The person you are working with may choose to change goals when she is faced with the reality of a situation. For example, the astronauts of Apollo 13 wanted to land on the moon until they began losing oxygen. At that point, they changed their goal to getting back to earth alive. As the coach, help the person be self-accountable for either doing what she said she wanted to do or deciding to change the plan.

In addition to the skills we have discussed for coaching, there are three other areas dealing with developing others that deserve attention: mentoring, using development resources wisely and coaching outside of work.

MENTORING

Mentoring is another way you can help develop people. Though there are many variations of mentoring, key components of a mentoring relationship often include the mentor taking a personal interest in her mentee's success, making herself available to answer questions or give advice upon request. Mentors often open up their network of influencers and access to opportunities the mentee would not otherwise have available. Many times, the mentee does not have a direct reporting relationship to the mentor. A mentor takes an active interest in the career development of her mentee and goes beyond the normal responsibilities of coaching.

> "You cannot teach a man anything. You can only help him to discover it within himself."
> – Galileo Galilei

In some instances, mentoring is focused on helping a young or new employee get acclimated to an organization and avoid pitfalls. Some companies also use "reverse mentoring," wherein a senior executive is paired with a younger employee to work toward a win-win goal: the executive helps the employee, and the employee teaches the executive some new technology and social media skills. The success of a mentor-mentee relationship depends largely on how well the two people get along; therefore, care should be taken before assigning people to that type of relationship. Some companies have a defined mentoring process, encouraging the integration of mentoring as a broader part of leadership, leadership development and the nurturing of a learning organization.

USE YOUR DEVELOPMENT RESOURCES WISELY

While coaching and mentoring are valuable ways for you to personally help develop others, make sure to take advantage of the other training and development resources available. The person you are coaching will benefit from workshops and other training within your organization or from outside vendors. To effectively use these resources, reread "Focus on Developing Your Strengths" in "1.0 Getting Started," and then apply that advice to those you are coaching. In summary, build on strengths rather than trying to fix weaknesses.

As a leader, your job is to help others recognize their natural talents and develop those into strengths, while acknowledging and neutralizing their weaknesses. In the best seller *Now, Discover Your Strengths*, Marcus Buckingham and Donald Clifton define natural talent as "any recurring patterns of thought, feeling or behavior that can be productively applied." They go on to define strengths as those actions you can perform near perfectly, over and over again.

Natural strengths do not equal developed strengths. For example, as a young boy, Ron was told he had a natural talent for playing the piano. There was only one problem: Ron did not enjoy practicing. Consequently, no one in their right minds would listen to Ron play the piano today and describe it as a strength. Potential does not guarantee performance. Potential plus practice (development) most often leads to superior performance.

Sending someone to a workshop to fix a weakness may result in some improvement, but it is not likely this person will be a top performer. It is much more likely he will be mediocre in using the talent. Though eliminating a weakness appears to be a useful goal when working with people, it does not return anywhere close to the benefits of developing a natural talent into a high-performing strength. When you develop a person's talent into a true strength (near-perfect, repeated performance) that person has the opportunity to be an "A" player and to strive toward "best in the world" status. Spend your resources on developing natural talent, not on trying to "fix" someone.

ORGANIZE AROUND STRENGTHS

Ideally, you should match people's talents to their job requirements during the recruiting process. When this is not possible, look for people with complementary strengths and organize them to help each other. For instance, if you have someone who struggles with interpersonal skills, perhaps her natural talent may be analysis of data or critical thinking. Let her do data analysis for someone who has interpersonal skills as a talent, and let the person with interpersonal skills take care of the relationship-building and communicating part of the job for the data analyzer. While this is not always possible, you will be surprised at what aligning peoples' skills with job requirements can do for a team's performance and satisfaction.

> "A great coach believes in you more than you do yourself, and she coaches you for performance based on potential."
> – Ron Price

Ron decided many years ago to quit trying to keep his files organized. Instead, he asks others who have a knack for filing to do it for him. It frees him up to focus on his strengths and gives others the work satisfaction of helping, based on their strengths. You can do something similar with the people you lead.

COACH OUTSIDE OF WORK

As mentioned at the beginning of this module, a coach is someone who helps the person being coached get the results she wants in a timely manner. Beyond your work role, coaching is a way to help a friend or family member who comes to you with a problem. Sometimes, you may not feel comfortable giving advice and, unless you are a licensed therapist, your advice is probably not as helpful as you would like to think it is. And yet, as a friend, you can help the other person think through her issue by using the four questions listed in the "Create Awareness" section of this module as the framework for a conversation.

Coaching is also a tool you can use for yourself. When you feel stymied by a situation, step back from it and ask yourself the four questions. Just keep in mind that most of us have blind spots. It may be helpful to get a friend or accountability partner to talk through the questions with you and help make sure you are being honest with yourself.

Coaching and developing others is a learnable skill, of which we touched on the basics in this module. To continue your learning, we invite you to visit our website at www.TheCompleteLeader.org to explore the resources available to help you become a better coach and mentor.

We have had the good fortune to be coaches for a number of people during our careers. Coaching is one of the most satisfying roles you can play in someone's life. The impact on them, and on you, is often far greater than you could imagine.

3.12

CUSTOMER FOCUS

WHAT IS CUSTOMER FOCUS?

Randy recently went into a tool warehouse store to buy some wedges to split wood. The following is his description of the transaction:

> I bought two wedges and some other items, and had estimated in my head that it would cost about $20. The store was busy. I worked my way to the cashier, who rang me up. My total was just over $30. I signed the tablet and gathered my stuff. Then, I realized that the total did not seem right. So, I checked the receipt to see what I missed. As it turned out, the wedges that I thought were $4.99 had been rung up at $9.99.
>
> I looked at the display again and, sure enough, they were marked $4.99. I went back and asked the clerk about the discrepancy. She was very polite and said right away, "Oh, we'll refund the difference." I suggested she come and look at the display, which we did. As it turned out, the $4.99 tags were for a different kind of wedge. The products had been mixed. I told her if the wedges were really $9.99, I was happy to pay. She said, "No, they're marked $4.99, and that's what we will

charge you." She went back to the register and called a manager to okay the refund.

The manager started to tell me how sometimes things get moved around, and the clerk spoke up and said, "No, these wedges were marked wrong." I was impressed by the clerk's obvious focus on the customer, even pushing back on her boss on my behalf. It was only ten dollars. However, my feeling now is that this is a store that values customers—even though that feeling is based on one encounter with one employee.

> **"The purpose of a business is to create a customer."**
>
> **– Peter Drucker**

We are sure you have stories about how you were either treated well or poorly when you were a customer. That is because we are all customers many times a day, in both big and small transactions. Each of these interactions is, in the words of Jan Carlzon, former president and CEO of Scandinavian Airlines System (SAS), a "moment of truth." You likely remember these encounters for a long time, and tell your friends about them—particularly the bad transactions.

In your many personal and professional roles, you respond to these moments of truth with your "customers" based on personal beliefs and values, and on the organizational rules and policies in use. Do you respond to customers with "caveat emptor," the Latin phrase meaning buyer beware? Do you invoke time limits or other conditions on a return policy? That is, are you looking out for the customer, or only looking out for your own needs?

The paradox is this: when you do not look out for your customers, this will eventually cause you to have problems. In short, lose-win becomes lose-lose.

WHY IS CUSTOMER FOCUS IMPORTANT?

Customers define value. If you watch an assembly line for an automobile, it is easy to see a car come together as it moves down the line. It gradually gains more value, until it is finally finished and sold at a dealership. No matter the business you are in, you are part of a similar assembly line: contributing value to some process or product that is leading to a final product or service. What this product or service is worth is determined by the person using it—the customer. As the supplier of the product or service, you know about your costs, but the customer gets to assign value, or worth. If your business is not providing sufficient value to cover costs, overhead and profit, you will not be in business for long. No margin, no mission.

Tomorrow's world is one of analytics, data mining, electronic patient records and even more shared personal information on social networks. This widespread, available data will allow for more individualized solutions to everything from manufacturing custom clothing on your own 3D printer at home to getting a cure for an illness that is tailored to a unique genetic code. A deep understanding of customers' needs—comprehending the uniqueness of each customer, and acting on it—will be a hallmark of top organizations. As a result, customization will become more universal, more intelligent and more technology-driven. All of these advances will come to those who have developed a consistent and skilled customer focus.

> "There is only one boss. The customer. And he can fire everybody in the company from the chairman on down, simply by spending his money somewhere else."
> – Sam Walton

Management expert Peter Drucker has said that seeing things as a customer or client would see them—what he called an "outside-in perspective"—is responsible for some of the most innovative businesses of the past and present. Think of iPods, Google and eBay, all innovative products and companies that understood a need that had not existed beforehand.

HOW IS CUSTOMER FOCUS LEARNED?

KNOW YOUR CUSTOMERS

We define a customer as anyone who receives a product or service from a supplier. If you publish a monthly report, whoever gets that report is your customer. If you are serving on a committee at church, the people who benefit from your committee work are your customers. Since every business serves both internal and external customers, everyone in the organization should understand how their work affects both those within the organization and the final, or external, customers. This customer "line of sight" also makes the work more meaningful and less abstract because you can see the benefits realized by the final customer.

FOCUS ON BASIC SKILLS

Maintaining a focus on customers is a complex skill made up of many of the more basic talents discussed in this book. Review the twenty-five competencies listed in the table of contents, and define, study, practice and promote the specific competencies needed for customer focus in your business. There is no one exact list, but we believe the following skills are critical and basic:

- Decision-making from Part One
- All the skills described in Part Two: self-management, personal accountability, flexibility, resilience and goal achievement

- Listening, diplomacy and tact, and interpersonal skills from Part Three

Review these competencies, add in any others that apply to your business, and think about how they can improve your customer focus.

BUILD STRONG RELATIONSHIPS

The essence of customer focus is building a relationship with your customers that they would like to continue. Again, relationships drive results. To build high trust relationships, focus on a combination of character and competence. Of course, leaders must be competent, and we hope the ideas in this book are helping build your leadership competencies. But your character—honesty, responsibility, trustworthiness and other traits—is also critical. These character traits are built or lost one day and one interaction at a time.

> "Rule #1: The customer is always right.
> Rule #2: If the customer is ever wrong, reread rule #1."
> – Stew Leonard

Take a moment to think about the companies you like to do business with. What are they doing to improve their relationship with you and other customers? How are the leaders in that company demonstrating competence and character, and can you learn from them?

To help build strong relationships with your own customers, try the following tips:

KEEP YOUR PROMISES

Make promises sparingly, and keep them rigorously. If you make promises without thinking, and then fail to keep them, it will lower the trust in a customer relationship—or any relationship, for that matter. Appointments, deadlines and responses are all examples of promises you make either explicitly or implicitly, and they should be taken seriously. Of course, occasionally something out of your control makes it impossible to keep a well-made promise. This is a great time to show your customer focus. At the least, apologize and take responsibility. It can also be a great opportunity for you to do something above and beyond to regain the customer's trust.

GO THE EXTRA MILE

Customers notice whether you are genuinely interested in helping them or are just "going through the motions." Think about when you ask someone in a retail store to help you find something, for example. You probably prefer if they say, "Let me show you where that is," and then walk you to it, rather than, "It's in aisle fourteen." The best of them also ask if you need a related item that you might have forgotten.

> "A satisfied customer is the best business strategy of all."
> – Michael LeBoeuf

Going the extra mile involves being helpful but also courteous and knowledgeable. This begins with how you treat those who follow you. Several experts on customer service teach that the way you treat your employees is ultimately the way they will treat your customers. Make sure your staff members have enough training, information and power to deal with reasonable customer issues. Enterprise Rent-A-Car employees can issue refunds or "make it right" with their customers on the spot if there is a problem with a rental car. They do not have to have a manager approve it. Their motto is, "We'll pick you up," which is another example of going the extra mile.

Note that some of the practices of going the extra mile, as well as customer focus in general, are implemented by individual people but supported by organizational processes and systems. It takes both systems and individuals to create and maintain a customer focus. What can you do in your company or department to implement processes and systems with a focus on both the internal and external customer?

PART 4:

LEADERS ARE AUTHENTIC

Each of the sections of this book has focused on leadership qualities: clear thinking, managing oneself and leading others. In combination with the companion website, www.TheCompleteLeader.org, we have given you the tools to develop yourself into the best version of yourself. But as you continue on your leadership journey, it is important to remember that the most powerful leadership quality is being authentically you. You are uniquely capable. Being able to develop greatness, without turning into something you are not, is the mark of a world-class leader.

In Part Four, we focus on just one competency: authenticity. This section offers a unique blending of the other twenty-four competencies as they specifically relate to you. The module is:

4.1 Authenticity – Ability to be the best possible version of you

Throughout this module, we deal with the fact that sometimes a job requires different skills than come naturally to an individual.

When there is a gap between what the job is asking for and who you are, it can be much more difficult to be authentic. One of the great fallacies of large organizations is that they believe leaders are developed by moving around from department to department. Unfortunately, this results in constantly trying to fit a square peg into a round hole for the sake of diversity or breadth of experience. These types of "leadership development" heighten the chance of mediocrity because there is never the chance to become someone who is one of a kind.

Inevitably, there will be a skill needed in your current position that does not come naturally to you. In an ideal world, you will find a perfect fit that does not require you to shift who you are. But if your position demands something outside your abilities, you can develop a "new authenticity."

We recognize that developing authenticity seems to go against the word's meaning of being genuine. However, think about how you arrived at who you are. There were a number of experiences that made up the person that is genuinely you. If there is an important skill you are lacking, you can work to develop that ability to grow yourself and your team—and, with enough practice, you will become what you practice. With time, that better version of yourself will become authentically you. Part Four focuses on discovering who you are and who you want to be—and then helping you get there.

AUTHENTICITY

WHAT IS AUTHENTICITY?

The title of Max DePree's classic book says it all: *Leadership Is an Art*. It is a creative endeavor. Like other artists, the leader creates himself while he builds the projects he envisions and brings into reality. M.C. Richards, the poet, potter and essayist, describes the creative spirit in all of us:

> The creative spirit creates with whatever materials are present. With food, with children, with building blocks, with speech, with thoughts, with pigment, with an umbrella, or a wine glass or a torch. We are not craftsmen only during studio hours. Any more than a man is wise only in his library. Or devout only in a church. The material is not the sign of the creative feeling for life: of the warmth and sympathy and reverence which foster being; techniques are not a sign; art is not the sign. The sign is the light that dwells within the act, whatever its nature or its medium.

Like other artists, a leader creates "with whatever materials are present." A leader's raw materials include strengths, talents, natural and learned values, and the talents of those whom he leads. And at the heart of that creativity is authenticity.

Authenticity means real or natural—not fake. Authentic people are true to their own personality, spirit or character. An effective leader, at the core, must be authentic. An authentic leader must learn how to be the best version of themselves, and be honest with themselves and their team about their weaknesses. It takes courage and a willingness to be vulnerable to openly admit to needing assistance in those areas of weakness—to ask for help. Therefore, leadership cannot be reduced to an equation, quick tips or even specific advice. Instead, focusing on developing authenticity is the foundation on which all of the other competencies are built.

At some point, a leader begins to understand who he is: his strengths, his personality, his way of being in the world. He understands that he takes this uniqueness with him as he practices his craft. Each person's leadership style and skills are organically grown, inside out, starting from who he is.

WHY IS AUTHENTICITY IMPORTANT?

Authenticity may be the most important leadership skill of all, because exhibiting authenticity is the foundation for trust. People do not want to follow a leader who is a fake—and too often, they can tell if you present a facade that is not true to your behavior.

Everyone comes equipped with a certain style—a "voice"—starting soon after birth. It is a gift—a starting point. Most importantly, it is not necessarily a *final* style. As you begin to develop your ultimate authentic style, you need to know what your present authentic self looks like and where the gaps exist between who you are and who you want to become.

For example, perhaps you describe yourself as very action-oriented, but the people who work for you describe you as impatient and blunt. You might protest that impatient and blunt is just "who you are" and, because you want to be authentic, people will have to deal with it. (And, if you are lucky enough to get such honest feedback, acknowledge it and thank those who gave it to you.)

At your retirement, if people show up, will they give you an auto-graphed baseball bat as a symbol of your leadership style? (Randy has heard of this happening.) While taking action is an important quality in a leader, when done without other skills like empathy and understanding others, its unintended consequences may offset the gain from the action. Taking action and being blunt and impa-tient are not the same.

In this example, although being action-oriented is a plus, it has a negative impact on others. Your strength becomes your weakness. Discoveries like this help identify gaps to work on: in this case, being action-oriented while remaining more patient. One of our colleagues, Steve Morris, taught us this valuable insight: "The one weakness we all share in common is a strength overused." In our modern vernacular, we describe this as, "when you are a hammer, everything starts to look like a nail." Authenticity doesn't mean letting go and just being who you are. Instead, it is a process of continuous learning and becoming the best version of yourself, which always needs to be understood in the context of your current roles, responsibilities, opportunities and challenges.

Always check the effectiveness of new actions for improvement by eliciting feedback from your team. If you are still getting the same comments in a few months, change your plan. Although being blunt and impatient may be "who you are," it is not helping you be an effective leader. By working to modify those qualities, you can choose to improve your authentic self to be more effective.

To evaluate your authenticity, ask yourself these questions:

- Am I comfortable with who I am, or am I trying to fake it?

- Am I being transparent?
- Am I open to feedback from others?

By definition, your path to authenticity will be unique. The idea is to be open to feedback on who you are now and how that differs from the leader you want to become.

HOW IS AUTHENTICITY LEARNED?

RECOGNIZE DEFINING MOMENTS

Be on the lookout for situations that will help you define your unique style. Typically, they will not look like opportunities, but they are. These defining moments will appear at just the wrong times: when you are stressed; when someone questions your decision or authority; when you are scared because you do not know what solution to choose; when there is too much to do and not enough time to do it; when your leadership role butts heads with the other roles in your life; when a flight is cancelled or a critical meeting is postponed; or when the car battery is dead and you are late for your son's soccer game. These are the true practice fields for authenticity. Think about the last time you were in one of these types of situations. Ask yourself, "How did I respond?" and "Does my response reflect who I want to be?"

Those instances, when you are out of your comfort zone and short on personal resources, will clearly show you how far you have come and where your work still needs to be done. As we have recommended throughout the book, it is always helpful to have someone, in addition to yourself, observe your behaviors. Ask a friend, colleague or family member to give you feedback on how you respond in moments of stress. This invaluable person needs to know what you are working on, and he must be able to give you the unvarnished truth about how your behavior is impacting others.

BE COURAGEOUS

Change involves courage. It involves taking chances and experiencing the consequences of behaving differently. As you go down this path of personal development, you will be changing your thinking and behavior. You will not be able to rely on old habits that you have outgrown.

> **"You don't have to hold a position in order to be a leader."**
> **– Henry Ford**

Think about a time when you did something courageous. When you acted bravely, what made it worth the risk? Why did you take the action? Our guess is it had to do with something you felt strongly about. Perhaps you agonized over it for some time before acting, running through the worst-case scenarios in your mind. When you finally made the decision, you likely felt better and relieved. You probably wished you had acted sooner. You may have felt the way Anaïs Nin did when she said, "And the day came when the risk to remain tight in a bud was more painful than the risk it took to blossom."

This is the pattern and process you will go through time and again on your way to authentic leadership. It is the path to growth. What makes changing worth the risk? Transformation is the only path available; we know of no shortcut. You cannot fake authenticity.

Taking the risk also makes similar decisions to choose new directions easier to make. Your self-efficacy will have increased—in essence, enlarging your comfort zone. Many of the stressful or difficult situations that may have pushed your buttons before will not have the same power over you. You will be operating at a more authentic level by becoming a greater expression of your potential.

GET IN THE LEADERSHIP PERFORMANCE ZONE

People talk about athletes and artists being "in the zone" when they are fully engaged with some task and performing at a high level. You can also be "in the zone" as an authentic leader. If you have already had that experience of performing in your zone, you can focus on increasing those moments in your leadership.

The pros we marvel at on TV did not start out at their present expertise. As they were learning their craft, their peak performance zone gradually improved. This peak performance zone is described as a middle ground, with boredom below it and overload or panic above it; it is not the same as your comfort zone. The only way to grow your leadership performance zone is to challenge it and push against it. That is why you take the risks—because those who do not risk do not grow. They will be the people whose authentic selves have never fully emerged through this growth process.

A word of warning: taking the path of authenticity, and regularly getting in the zone, may cause you to become overly courageous and confident. More courage and confidence would seem to be a good thing, but always look for the balance of opposites. If your courage and confidence grow without being balanced by humility, you will fall prey to another of the leadership traps: narcissism, or becoming a legend in your own mind. This messiah complex will undermine all your good, courageous work.

BE OPEN AND ACKNOWLEDGE OTHERS

No one is perfect. And yet, for some reason, many people do not feel good enough for the positions they are in. As a result, leaders tend to hide weaknesses and act as if they are flawless. Paradoxically, people who act authentically, letting their imperfections show and admitting that they do not have all the answers, generate more loyalty, not less. Perfectionism is one of the biggest detriments to authenticity. It is difficult to be "real" when you feel the need to be perfect.

Remember, too, that few things of substance are created entirely by one person. Praise is not a zero-sum commodity, so spread it around liberally. Encourage your followers to be courageous and improve their own self-efficacy. Elevate everyone to a higher level. Go from "I am great" to "we are great."

Randy was lunching with an excellent leader who was one of four finalists for the National Person of the Year award in his field. It was a big honor, and one this leader deserved. He was going to Washington, DC, to be wined, dined and interviewed by various media. During lunch, Randy's friend mentioned that he was getting some coaching on how to field questions from the press, but he was not comfortable with the coaching he was getting. His coaches were advising him to have ready answers as to what he had done to be selected as a national finalist. Yet, his whole leadership style was about creating a team and focusing on what the whole team had accomplished. One of his coaches would ask a question, and he would automatically answer, "This is what we did…" He was getting frustrated with them and they with him. Randy suggested that authenticity never goes out of style, and if the leader answered authentically, he would be fine. We suggest a similar focus on authenticity in your own leadership.

THINK, DO AND RELATE AUTHENTICALLY

In *The Complete Leader,* we have explored three important dimensions for leaders: thinking, doing (getting results) and relating (being with others). We have given definitions, suggestions and stories, as ways to help you consider how to be more effective in each of the three dimensions; it is up to you to experiment with these ideas and learn from experience. Every leader works in all three dimensions, and you will think, act and relate somewhat differently than others as you develop your own authentic leadership style. What follows are some ways to develop authenticity in these dimensions.

THINK AUTHENTICALLY

Thinking refers to the mental process of imagining and understanding yourself and the world around you. It includes considering your current roles and your future: what you want to create and achieve, as well as the systems, cultures and people you deal with. In essence, you go through the world and life being guided by a movie that is playing in only one theatre—the one between your ears.

Thinking authentically means doing the mental work it takes to know what you stand for as a person and leader. Ask yourself, "What is my philosophy of leadership?" The easiest place to start answering this is by creating a clear and positive vision of your future as a leader. You need to be able to describe that future in enough detail that you know it when you see it. It often helps to write it down, reflect on it, and then add more detail and conviction. It has been said that the best way to create the future you want is to envision it. Call on your imagination much more than your memory. In *The Fifth Discipline*, author Peter Senge defines personal mastery as the "discipline of continually clarifying and deepening our personal vision, of focusing our energies, of developing patience, and of seeing reality objectively." It is the discipline of becoming an authentic leader.

> "Authenticity is the alignment of head, mouth, heart, and feet—thinking, saying, feeling, and doing the same thing—consistently. This builds trust, and followers love leaders they can trust."
>
> – Lance Secretan

Once you have a clear picture of the type of authentic leader you want to become, you will likely see where you fall short. But you can close those gaps between where you are now and the self you envision. Reaching your desired future takes a commitment to long-term learning. You cannot be satisfied with your current state of expertise. Instead, expand your performance zone.

As you start this journey toward growth, you will notice that the pace of change is increasing. Ask yourself, "How will I keep up with the changes in the areas that are crucial to my leadership?" and "How much time am I committing to my own improvement?" To put it into perspective, think about how much time and preparation, day in and day out, a world-class athlete spends getting ready to compete. If your goal is to be a world-class leader, what should be the ratio of time you spend preparing versus performing (doing your day-to-day work)? It is in the preparation where you expand your zone of performance.

> "I believe God made me for a purpose, but he also made me fast. When I run, I feel His pleasure."
> – Eric Liddell, *Chariots of Fire*

This preparation does not have to be a week of formal training at Harvard, although there is nothing wrong with that. The key is to be interested—dare we say *passionate*—about what you are creating. When you decide to *become* an expert in your field, any number of opportunities to learn will present themselves. Then, determine the appropriate amount of time you will devote to improving yourself while continuing to keep all your other commitments.

Even if you do not feel you can take time away to study something you are passionate about, we suggest committing thirty minutes a day to it. Anyone can find thirty minutes every day to do something important. Get up earlier, give up half an hour of TV, eliminate thirty minutes a day of time wasters at work. Thirty minutes a day for 365 days is 182.5 hours, or just over seven and a half days. By making a simple adjustment to your schedule, you can gain an extra week's worth of learning. When you are thinking about preparing for your future, also refer to "1.5 Continuous Learning" and to our website, www.TheCompleteLeader.org, for more suggestions.

Thinking about your own future and legacy is necessary but not sufficient. Effective leaders also consider their own roles within the context of what they are trying to achieve, given the constraints of the larger systems. Your organization, competition, government regulations, the communities you do business with, and the world at large all present challenges and opportunities. An effective leader must have a long-term vision and strategy while being aware of the day-to-day issues.

Finally, remember that the "truth" you have is your truth, not The Truth. As we have discussed in this module and previous ones, each person sees the world based on her own mental filters, as a movie playing only in that person's head. Your truth is almost always partial and biased. Knowing the difference between "this is the way it is" and "this is the way I am thinking about it" is crucial to growth. Growth requires being open to having your assumptions challenged and your mind changed. You must be willing to collaborate with others to get beyond your own perspective. Thinking authentically does not mean that you give up your own view of the world. It does mean that you realize your view is partial, and you are willing to broaden your thinking based on the ideas of others.

DO AUTHENTICALLY

It has been said that leadership begins with a vision and ends with results. Effective leaders get things done with and through others while also working to improve their own competencies and ways of achieving results. This takes a balance of thinking and doing. Both are necessary, and neither is sufficient by itself. Too much thinking leads to "paralysis by analysis." On the other hand, action without thought and focus creates a lot of motion but not a lot of progress. Effective leadership strikes the right balance between the two.

Everyone has a preferred ratio of thinking to action. Some people are thoughtful and slow to act; others are more action-oriented. No one style works in all situations, so it is important to be aware of your own style and clearly evaluate your present reality. Discern what balance of thinking and action is called for, and then adapt your behavior to move your vision forward.

As discussed in the previous section, you must first figure out your leadership philosophy and create a clear vision of the future. Then, authentic doing comes in. Authentic doing is speaking and acting congruently with who you are choosing to become. Using the earlier example, let us say you are choosing to be more patient in your dealings with others and less blunt and rude. In this case, authentic doing would be acting in a more patient way toward others. If you do lose your patience or speak in a rude way toward others and realize you are not being the person you want to be, authentically apologize. It is okay to not be perfect. Remember: perfectionism thwarts authenticity.

When you are acting authentically, there is congruence between what you are thinking, saying and doing. As Oscar Wilde said, "Be yourself. Everyone else is taken." Do not try to be someone else. Instead, attempt to live toward the vision of yourself in the future. You are not static and unchangeable. You are capable of changing and growing throughout your life.

Once you have thought about what the "best you" looks like, authentic doing is supported by asking yourself, "How would the 'best me' spend her time this week?" Then, use your response to create an ideal weekly plan. When it does not turn out as planned (and it will not), go back and review your calendar. Ask yourself the following questions:

- What unexpected things happened this week?

- What can I do to minimize or prevent them from happening in the future?

- What time-wasters kept me from my best this week? Are they a part of who I want to be?

- Am I wasting time on activities that do not seem necessary to or consistent with developing my authentic self?

- Could I be sabotaging my own growth?

- How can I reduce or eliminate those time-wasters in the future?

- Am I clear about the most important roles in my life? (There is more to a life well lived than work.)

- How can I be my authentic self next week?

Asking these questions of yourself, and honestly answering them, is another way to apply the Plan-Do-Check-Act cycle of continuous improvement to your leadership in all of life (see "Plan-Do-Check-Act" under "1.3 Planning and Organization" for more on this process).

There was an excellent CEO who lived in Randy's community and who embodied the work-life balance of doing authentically. This man was head of a large corporation. As expected, he served on a number of boards, was active in the community and was devoted to his family. He also wrote and performed music. He formed and ran a band that played regularly, often to support nonprofit agencies. When he left to head up a larger corporation in another part of the nation, those in the community missed him on many fronts, not just as a CEO.

When was he his most authentic self? Was he a CEO who wrote music, or was he a musician who happened to be a CEO? It is okay to be both. As you consider creating your authentic self, do not limit your creativity to one role. We all have passions. To the extent that you can incorporate your passions into the roles in your life, you begin to live more of a "want to" life and less of a "have to" life. Ask yourself, "What am I passionate about?" and "Am I giving those passions enough energy and time?"

RELATE AUTHENTICALLY

The third dimension of relating, or being with people, is an important focus as you begin leading authentically. Since leadership is by definition a group activity, leaders will always be working with people. It follows that effective leaders have a clear understanding and appreciation of others.

Think of relating as the outer ring of three concentric circles. The inner circle is the thinking circle, and the middle circle is the doing circle, which also includes thinking. The largest circle, encompassing the other two, is the relating circle—the people dimension.

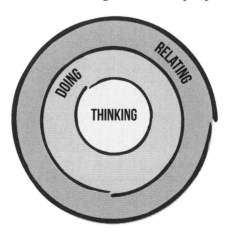

As Dr. Robert Hartman, father of formal axiology (the study of values), pointed out many years ago, "Things are more valuable than ideas or concepts, and people are more valuable than things." To be an effective long-term leader, it is important to be clear about all three dimensions, with relating being the most important. When you are thinking and behaving (doing) authentically, you will relate with others in an authentic way.

Continuing the previous example of becoming more patient in your dealings with others, an authentic way to relate could be to tell those you work with what your intention is. Then, ask them to please tell you when they think you are being impatient or rude. Of course, when they do this, you must respond in a patient and polite way. Say something like, "Thanks for your feedback. This isn't easy for me, but it is important to me. I will use your feedback. Keep it coming."

As you continue to define and create your leadership style, follow the ancient aphorism, "Know thyself." Get clear about your preferred thinking, doing and relating styles. Make sure your styles serve you well and are not defaults from the past. Ask yourself, "Am I comfortable with who I am, or am I trying to fake it?" Once you create awareness, you can choose to embrace the styles or change and improve them, if needed.

Be authentic. Be yourself. Authenticity is a choice you can always make. It is the most important leadership work for you to do, and the most rewarding.

CONCLUSION

GREAT LEADERS FOCUS ON THE "WHY"

Throughout this book, you have been developing skills unique to your leadership journey. The focus of our work has been on the "what" and "how" of developing those competencies. As we conclude this book and you continue on your journey, we want to remind you that there is a deeper aspect to leadership. It is the character, purpose, guiding beliefs or ethos that underpins the "what" and "how" of great leadership. It is the "why."

The ethos of *The Complete Leader* may be best understood by examining how it supports the four dimensions of leadership: leaders are clear thinkers, leaders lead themselves, leaders lead others and leaders are authentic.

Great leaders recognize that growth doesn't have a finish line. Instead, it is a spiral of upward maturity and discovery. As the title of Simon Sinek's best-selling book states, great leaders always "start with why." They think clearly about purpose. They are compelled by an intrinsic ownership of motive that extends beyond tangible rewards. In some particular way, they want to "make a dent in the universe," as Steve Jobs put it. Their motivation isn't necessarily to impress others. Instead, they can be motivated to love their families more fully, serve their communities quietly, or cure the incurable. What is important is the drive to continuously clarify "why," gaining new insights and momentum along the way.

"He who has a why can endure any how." Friedrich Nietzsche's quote summarizes how the "why" of leadership helps leaders lead themselves. When someone has a clear and positive goal in his mind—an inspiring future to move toward—it provides the power to motivate him today. The compelling "why" is the catalyst that turns problems into opportunities and allows leaders to persevere and overcome seemingly insurmountable roadblocks.

World-class leaders inspire others to make commitments they might not otherwise make. How does this happen? It is the power of the "why." As leaders share their purpose with others, the mental energy created by the vision of that positive future infuses others with the desire to be a part of something worthwhile. When people become excited about the prospects of creating something worthy of their time and energy, they tend to work because they want to, not because they have to.

The "why" of leadership allows great leaders to transcend self-interest and self-promotion. They are captivated by something bigger, more fulfilling—to serve a people or a purpose greater than themselves. Though they could rightfully conclude, because of personal achievements, "I am great," they see beyond this private victory and reach for the public victory of, "We are great!" With informed humility, they see themselves as part of a greater whole.

As you work to build the competencies detailed in this book, our desire is that you will continue to:

- Increase your clarity of thought, yet always remain open-minded to new insights,

- Grow in your mastery of self-management, yet be patient and understanding while falling short of perfection,

- Change destinies through leading others, while remaining open to being changed through their influence and examples, and

- Discover and manifest your uniquely authentic leadership purpose while maintaining the humility to honor the same in others.

We hope you will treat this book and our website as your constant companion throughout your leadership journey.

APPENDIX 1

SELF-ASSESSMENT FOR THE 25 LEADERSHIP COMPETENCIES

The purpose of this self-assessment is to gather data to help you reflect on your journey toward becoming a complete leader. By adding up your scores in each section, you have an opportunity to measure yourself against a high standard of excellence. Each leader's degree of self-awareness will vary, with some leaders over-valuing their current levels of mastery and others undervaluing their skills. The overall scores are not as important as the patterns that emerge. These patterns will help you recognize your current strengths and where you may benefit by giving more attention to future development.

This assessment is also available online at www.TheCompleteLeader.org in the subscription section.

When you complete the assessment online, your results will be tabulated automatically. Additional resources are also available to help you continue on your leadership journey.

LEADERS ARE CLEAR THINKERS

1.1 FUTURISTIC THINKING

I seem to have the ability to "look around the corner" to see the future in ways others don't.

	1	2	3	4	5

Never   Always

I regularly read about future trends and think about their impact on my work.

	1	2	3	4	5

Never   Always

I can name at least three friends or associates I regularly meet with who are great futuristic thinkers.

	1	2	3	4	5

Never   Always

When facing decisions about the future, I construct and consider a variety of possible scenarios.

	1	2	3	4	5

Never   Always

I periodically write detailed descriptions about what the future may look like in my organization.

	1	2	3	4	5

Never   Always

Total score for Futuristic Thinking: _____

CONCEPTUAL THINKING

I enjoy discussing concepts, paradigms and business philosophies with my associates and friends.

	1	2	3	4	5	
Never						Always

I look for and identify the underlying assumptions behind organizational strategies.

	1	2	3	4	5	
Never						Always

I think about the models, concepts and principles that I find in the world around me and how they relate to my leadership opportunities.

	1	2	3	4	5	
Never						Always

I have a list of conceptual models or organizing principles that I use regularly in my leadership and share with others.

	1	2	3	4	5	
Never						Always

I think about the advantages and disadvantages of the structure and culture in my organization and how I can influence it for better outcomes.

	1	2	3	4	5	
Never						Always

Total score for Conceptual Thinking: _____

PLANNING AND ORGANIZATION

I have a list of "big picture" goals for what I want to accomplish, both personally and professionally.

	1	2	3	4	5	
Never						Always

I regularly set and achieve SMART goals (Specific, Measurable, Achievable, Relevant, Time-bound).

	1	2	3	4	5	
Never						Always

I have a current and detailed SLOT analysis (Strengths, Limitations, Opportunities, Threats) for my organizational responsibilities.

	1	2	3	4	5	
Never						Always

I use tools to help me prioritize my short- and long-term goals.

	1	2	3	4	5	
Never						Always

I complete a plan before beginning a project.

	1	2	3	4	5	
Never						Always

Total score for Planning and Organization: _____

CREATIVITY

I enjoy brainstorming and "out-of-the-box" thinking with others.

	1	2	3	4	5	
Never						Always

I find it easy to suspend judgment in the initial stages of exploring new possibilities.

	1	2	3	4	5	
Never						Always

I have a specific process for creative thinking when facing new challenges.

	1	2	3	4	5	
Never						Always

I have been part of, or led, a creative thinking session to develop something new in the past sixty days.

	1	2	3	4	5	
Never						Always

I regularly come up with new ideas for improving results.

	1	2	3	4	5	
Never						Always

Total Score for Creativity: _____

CONTINUOUS LEARNING

Those around me consider me an expert in a specific field related to my work.

         1   2   3   4   5

Never   Always

I have a defined professional development plan for the next twelve months or longer.

         1   2   3   4   5

Never   Always

I read from thought leaders in my fields of interest for at least three hours per week.

         1   2   3   4   5

Never   Always

I have attended two or more off-site professional development learning opportunities (conferences, forums, seminars, etc.) in the past year.

         1   2   3   4   5

Never   Always

I actively support others in their quest to learn.

         1   2   3   4   5

Never   Always

Total score for Continuous Learning: _____

PROBLEM-SOLVING

I enjoy dissecting a problem and developing a step-by-step plan to resolve it.

      1   2   3   4   5

Never   Always

I am intrigued by "unsolvable" problems and don't mind the ambiguity of complex, multi-faceted challenges.

      1   2   3   4   5

Never   Always

I regularly ask several "why" questions when seeking to understand the relevance and context of a problem.

      1   2   3   4   5

Never   Always

When studying a problem, I consistently work to separate assumptions from facts.

      1   2   3   4   5

Never   Always

After "solving" a problem, I regularly track the results of my solution in order to keep improving more on the results.

      1   2   3   4   5

Never   Always

Total score for Problem-Solving: _____

DECISION-MAKING

I find it easy to make the right decision at the right time for optimal results.

	1	2	3	4	5	
Never						Always

I recognize which decisions are mine to make and which decisions should be delegated to someone else.

	1	2	3	4	5	
Never						Always

I write down the significant decisions I make and review the results of these decisions nine to twelve months later.

	1	2	3	4	5	
Never						Always

I have a specific decision-making process I utilize when making decisions with long-term or significant impact.

	1	2	3	4	5	
Never						Always

I approach important decisions with a mix of approximately 60 percent intuition and 40 percent data analysis.

	1	2	3	4	5	
Never						Always

Total score for Decision-Making: _____

Total score for Clear Thinking: _____

LEADERS LEAD THEMSELVES

2.1 SELF-MANAGEMENT

I maintain a good balance between taking care of myself physically and emotionally and getting my work completed on time.

	1	2	3	4	5	
Never						Always

I am always conscious of managing my response to how I react to people and situations.

	1	2	3	4	5	
Never						Always

I have a clear understanding of priorities and what matters most in my work.

	1	2	3	4	5	
Never						Always

I can work independently without direct supervision to accomplish goals.

	1	2	3	4	5	
Never						Always

I am able to maintain a relaxed focus and "present moment awareness" throughout my workday without periods of hyperactivity or low energy.

	1	2	3	4	5	
Never						Always

Total score for Self-Management: _____

2.2 PERSONAL ACCOUNTABILITY

I do not make excuses or blame others when I fail to deliver on a commitment.

	1	2	3	4	5	
Never						Always

I do what needs to be done without getting distracted by lesser points.

	1	2	3	4	5	
Never						Always

I take the responsibility to know and negotiate the expectations others have toward me and to ask for specific feedback.

	1	2	3	4	5	
Never						Always

I accept responsibility for my emotions, behaviors and results.

	1	2	3	4	5	
Never						Always

I learn from my mistakes and failures to help me improve performance with future assignments.

	1	2	3	4	5	
Never						Always

Total score for Personal Accountability: _____

2.3 FLEXIBILITY

I recognize changing circumstances and adjust my tactics in order to achieve the optimal results.

	1	2	3	4	5	
Never						Always

I resist the temptation to insist on doing things my way when people ask me to consider alternatives.

	1	2	3	4	5	
Never						Always

I am comfortable living with a certain amount of ambiguity in circumstances, while not losing my focus on my goals and desired results.

	1	2	3	4	5	
Never						Always

I take reasonable risks and learn from both failure and success.

	1	2	3	4	5	
Never						Always

I am willing to change directions, priorities and schedules when circumstances dictate it wise to do so.

	1	2	3	4	5	
Never						Always

Total score for Flexibility: _____

2.4 RESILIENCY

I have experienced and recovered from one or more significant setbacks in my career and/or personal life.

	1	2	3	4	5	
Never						Always

I reflect on setbacks, failures and heartache, looking for opportunities that will yield benefits.

	1	2	3	4	5	
Never						Always

I discuss tough problems with friends and associates.

	1	2	3	4	5	
Never						Always

I bounce back quickly from tough days with optimism that things will get better soon.

	1	2	3	4	5	
Never						Always

I engage in various activities weekly that provide personal renewal and recovery from the day-to-day stresses of work and life.

	1	2	3	4	5	
Never						Always

Total score for Resiliency: _____

2.5 GOAL ACHIEVEMENT

I have a set of written goals for my personal and professional life.

        1   2   3   4   5

Never   Always

I take action quickly to accomplish my goals.

        1   2   3   4   5

Never   Always

I have strategies and specific processes I use to accomplish my professional and personal goals.

        1   2   3   4   5

Never   Always

I share my goals with one or more associates or friends as a way to be accountable for results.

        1   2   3   4   5

Never   Always

I track my results and achieve 80 percent or more of my written goals.

        1   2   3   4   5

Never   Always

Total score for Goal Achievement: _____

Total score for Leading Oneself: _____

LEADERS LEAD OTHERS

3.1 EMPATHY

I consistently listen to understand others and their underlying emotions.

        1   2   3   4   5

Never   Always

I find it easy to set aside my assumptions about others so I can understand them at deeper levels of insight.

        1   2   3   4   5

Never   Always

When listening to others, I repeat back their facts and reflect the feelings I am hearing to verify what they are communicating.

        1   2   3   4   5

Never   Always

My conversations are a balance of asking meaningful questions and stating my thoughts.

        1   2   3   4   5

Never   Always

I volunteer for a nonprofit group that helps those in need at least once a month.

        1   2   3   4   5

Never   Always

Total score for Empathy: _____

3.2 UNDERSTANDING AND EVALUATING OTHERS

I reject stereotyping others based on their ethnicity, functional responsibilities, beliefs, age, gender or personalities and see each person as unique.

	1	2	3	4	5	
Never						Always

I consistently lead and support others by focusing on their talents and how to leverage those talents to achieve professional and organizational success.

	1	2	3	4	5	
Never						Always

I seek to understand multiple perspectives around important issues.

	1	2	3	4	5	
Never						Always

I know the names and interests of my associates' spouses, close friends and children.

	1	2	3	4	5	
Never						Always

I have copies of talent profiles for those I work with and use the profiles regularly to work effectively with my colleagues.

	1	2	3	4	5	
Never						Always

Total score for Understanding and Evaluating Others: _____

3.3 PRESENTING SKILLS

I look forward to opportunities to give formal presentations.

	1	2	3	4	5	
Never						Always

I have completed one or more training courses on presentation skills.

	1	2	3	4	5	
Never						Always

I demonstrate a strong leadership presence in the way I dress, engage others in conversation, organize my workspace, and participate as an audience member in business presentations.

	1	2	3	4	5	
Never						Always

I find it easy to be organized and enthusiastic in the presentations I give.

	1	2	3	4	5	
Never						Always

Before giving a formal presentation, I always check all of the technical details that will influence my audience (sound, lights, equipment, etc.).

	1	2	3	4	5	
Never						Always

Total score for Presenting Skills: _____

3.4 WRITTEN COMMUNICATION

I proofread everything I write (including SMS messages, e-mail, etc.) before sending or publishing it.

	1	2	3	4	5	
Never						Always

I wait one day before sending written messages that are complex or emotional.

	1	2	3	4	5	
Never						Always

I strive to follow the rules of grammar, punctuation and spelling to ensure my writing is professional (including the use of spell-check or similar tools).

	1	2	3	4	5	
Never						Always

I avoid using jargon or colloquialisms in my writing unless I'm sure my intended audience is familiar with them.

	1	2	3	4	5	
Never						Always

I regularly write in a variety of mediums (journaling, essays, reports, articles, etc.) to improve my written communication skills.

	1	2	3	4	5	
Never						Always

Total score for Written Communication: _____

3.5 DIPLOMACY AND TACT

I am always polite and courteous toward others, regardless of their positions or attitudes toward me.

	1	2	3	4	5	
Never						Always

Others have commented that I am able to disagree without being disagreeable.

	1	2	3	4	5	
Never						Always

In conversations, I stay aware of what I am saying and doing and how I am being received.

	1	2	3	4	5	
Never						Always

I regularly ask for specific feedback from others about how I can be more tactful.

	1	2	3	4	5	
Never						Always

I am comfortable being respectful toward others, while maintaining my commitment to resolving difficult issues, without intimidating or being intimidated.

	1	2	3	4	5	
Never						Always

Total score for Diplomacy and Tact: _____

3.6 INTERPERSONAL SKILLS

I am not easily angered by others.

	1	2	3	4	5	
Never						Always

I enjoy knowing and working with people from diverse backgrounds, beliefs and experiences.

	1	2	3	4	5	
Never						Always

I find it easy to establish new relationships that are substantive and mutually beneficial.

	1	2	3	4	5	
Never						Always

I maintain some type of database of key relationships, and I review it regularly to consider how we can help and support each other.

	1	2	3	4	5	
Never						Always

I am aware of the value inherent in asking questions and affirming others.

	1	2	3	4	5	
Never						Always

Total score for Interpersonal Skills: _____

3.7 PERSUASION

I am willing to use my influence to persuade others based on my convictions.

	1	2	3	4	5	
Never						Always

I intentionally build trust (rather than intimidate, coerce or pull rank) as the foundation for effective persuasion.

	1	2	3	4	5	
Never						Always

I generally have a high level of credibility with others that makes persuasion easier to achieve.

	1	2	3	4	5	
Never						Always

When seeking to persuade others, I use both carefully developed logic and passion or conviction.

	1	2	3	4	5	
Never						Always

I am transparent in persuading others, and I do not manipulate or use tricks to gain their agreement.

	1	2	3	4	5	
Never						Always

Total score for Persuasion: _____

3.8 NEGOTIATION

I am able to separate people from issues when engaging in important negotiations.

	1	2	3	4	5	
Never						Always

I regularly seek win-win outcomes when negotiating with others.

	1	2	3	4	5	
Never						Always

I approach negotiations with the belief that there may be additional alternatives that are better than my current solutions.

	1	2	3	4	5	
Never						Always

I am able to maintain a positive, respectful attitude when negotiating with someone who takes an opposing position.

	1	2	3	4	5	
Never						Always

I listen thoroughly to understand the interests and issues of the parties with whom I negotiate.

	1	2	3	4	5	
Never						Always

Total score for Negotiation: _____

3.9 CONFLICT MANAGEMENT

I look for differing values or interests in conflicted parties to understand why the conflict exists.

	1	2	3	4	5	
Never						Always

I view conflicts as opportunities to gain deeper insights into others that may result in stronger cooperation in the future.

	1	2	3	4	5	
Never						Always

When addressing conflict, I take the time to understand and respond to emotions before addressing the facts.

	1	2	3	4	5	
Never						Always

I do not ignore or avoid conflict, and I seek to use conflict as a positive opportunity to strengthen relationships.

	1	2	3	4	5	
Never						Always

I welcome ideological conflict (debate) as a way to sharpen and improve decision-making skills.

	1	2	3	4	5	
Never						Always

Total score for Conflict Management: _____

3.10 TEAMWORK

I enjoy working as part of a team of individuals with diverse talents, backgrounds and interests.

	1	2	3	4	5

Never   Always

I look for opportunities to proactively contribute to the success of the teams I am a part of.

	1	2	3	4	5

Never   Always

I make it a priority to be accountable to the other members of the teams I am a part of.

	1	2	3	4	5

Never   Always

I actively participate in ideological debate about team decisions; once decisions are made, I give my full support to the implementation of those decisions.

	1	2	3	4	5

Never   Always

I do not talk about my team members differently or disparagingly when they are not present.

	1	2	3	4	5

Never   Always

Total score for Teamwork: _____

3.11 EMPLOYEE DEVELOPMENT AND COACHING

I have a professional development plan that includes being coachable and seeking specific feedback from others.

	1	2	3	4	5	
Never						Always

I have developed and regularly use the coaching skills of providing clear expectations, giving timely and effective feedback, and asking questions that help those I lead develop clarity and accountability.

	1	2	3	4	5	
Never						Always

I help others think more clearly about what they want, what they are currently doing, whether their current plan is working, and what they should change in order to improve their results.

	1	2	3	4	5	
Never						Always

I help those I coach increase their personal accountability to the commitments they have made.

	1	2	3	4	5	
Never						Always

I am actively involved in mentoring two or more people, helping them leverage their natural talents and navigate the unique opportunities or challenges in the organizations where they serve.

	1	2	3	4	5	
Never						Always

Total score for Development and Coaching: _____

3.12 CUSTOMER FOCUS

I ask my key customers, whether internal or external, how I'm doing and what I can do to improve.

	1	2	3	4	5	
Never						Always

I make promises to my customers sparingly and then keep them rigorously.

	1	2	3	4	5	
Never						Always

I consciously look for opportunities to exceed my customers' expectations by going the extra mile, particularly when it is unexpected.

	1	2	3	4	5	
Never						Always

I receive unsolicited referrals or endorsements from my customers, whether internal or external.

	1	2	3	4	5	
Never						Always

I intentionally develop new skills that will create value for my current and future customers.

	1	2	3	4	5	
Never						Always

Total score for Customer Focus: _____

Total score for Leading Others: _____

LEADERS ARE AUTHENTIC

4.1 AUTHENTICITY

I make career choices based on a clear understanding of my natural talents, developed strengths and weaknesses.

1	2	3	4	5

Never   Always

I am courageous when taking on new assignments or making significant career decisions, knowing that change ignites growth.

1	2	3	4	5

Never   Always

I clearly see how my success is dependent on the support and talent of those around me.

1	2	3	4	5

Never   Always

I have a clear mental picture of the "best me," and I follow this picture in the way I think, act and relate.

1	2	3	4	5

Never   Always

In my pursuit of becoming a complete leader, I am authentic with those outside of work in the way I think, act and relate.

1	2	3	4	5

Never   Always

Total score for Authentic Leadership: _____

Percent of Total Score (25): _____

The Complete Leader **Totals**

    Clear Thinking: _____

    Leading Oneself: _____

    Leading Others: _____

    Authentic Leadership: _____

Total Score: _____

THE TRIMETRIX® HD TALENT AND LEADERSHIP PROFILE

TriMetrix® HD brings the four sciences of behaviors, motivators, acumen and competencies together in a validated, bias-free and fully integrated assessment.

BEHAVIORS

Behavioral research suggests that the most effective people are those who understand themselves well enough to develop strategies to meet the demands of their environment. This report measures an individual's natural and adapted styles in response to: problems and challenges; interaction with and influence on other people; the pace of change; and compliance with rules and procedures.

TriMetrix® HD tells you *how* you will perform.

MOTIVATORS

Knowledge of motivators helps explain why individuals do things. The Personal Motivation & Engagement report measures the relative prominence of six basic interests or motivators: theoretical, utilitarian, aesthetic, social, individualistic and traditional.

TriMetrix® HD illuminates what motivates your behavior.

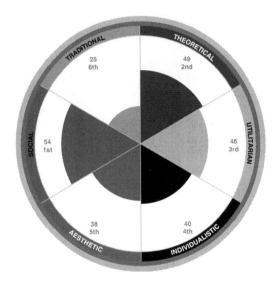

ACUMEN CAPACITY INDEX

The Acumen Indicators section is designed to help individuals understand how they analyze and interpret their experiences. A person's acumen, keenness, and depth of perception or discernment, is directly related to performance.

TriMetrix® HD explores both how your judgment impacts interaction with the external world and your own self-perception.

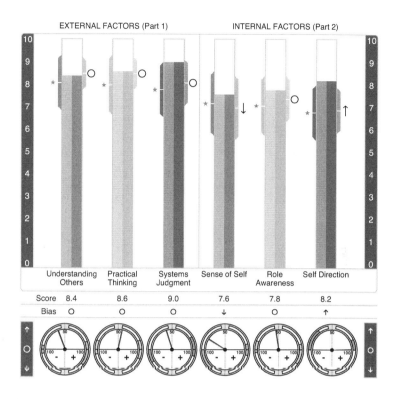

COMPETENCIES

An individual's hierarchy of competencies is key to success, and knowing what those competencies are is essential to reaching one's goals. This report is designed to assist in managing and developing an individual's career.

TriMetrix® HD describes *what* you have done in twenty-five research-based capacities related to the business environment.

TTI SUCCESS INSIGHTS®
DISCOVER • ENGAGE • ADVANCE • PERFORM

Development Indicator

This section of your report shows your development level of 25 personal skills based on your responses to the questionnaire. The 25 personal skills have been categorized into four levels; based on means and standard deviations. Well Developed, Developed, Moderately Developed and Needs Development.

	Personal Skills Ranking
1	Continuous Learning
2	Goal Achievement
3	Persuasion
4	Flexibility
5	Problem Solving Ability
6	Conceptual Thinking
7	Decision Making
8	Resiliency
9	Creativity
10	Personal Accountability
11	Futuristic Thinking
12	Negotiation
13	Employee Development/Coaching
14	Understanding & Evaluating Others
15	Teamwork
16	Self-Management
17	Customer Focus
18	Leadership
19	Conflict Management
20	Diplomacy & Tact
21	Presenting
22	Empathy
23	Interpersonal Skills
24	Written Communication
25	Planning & Organizing

Note: Don't be concerned if you have not developed all 25 personal skills. Research has proven that individuals seldom develop all 25. Development of the most important personal skills needed for your personal and professional life is what is critical.

■ Well Developed   ■ Developed   ■ Moderately Developed   □ Needs Development

Andrew Doe
Copyright © 2006-2013. Target Training International, Ltd.   5

You deserve the best, most insightful tools to understand your natural talent and how to develop yourself as The Complete Leader. To find out how you can complete the TriMetrix® HD Leadership Profile and review it with a certified professional talent analyst, write to us at support@TheCompleteLeader.org.

For more information and to view a sample leadership profile, visit us at www.TheCompleteLeader.org.

TriMetrix® is a registered trademark of Target Training International, Ltd.

ACKNOWLEDGMENTS

We have been surrounded by a tremendous amount of talent, teamwork and friendship throughout the writing of this book. This project started almost four years ago and because of our intent to continually expand the content through www.TheCompleteLeader.org, it will never be finished!

First, we are indebted to our publishing team from Aloha Publishing, including: Maryanna Young, Stacy Ennis, Hannah Cross, Cari Campbell, Fusion Creative Works and Sherri Lisnenbach. Their patience, commitment, tenacity and suggestions have contributed immensely to the book. The Aloha team has also collaborated with our web designers from Tribute Media, including Corey Smith and Don Elliott. This collaboration has been critical to our goal of providing a paradigm and gathering place for great leaders. We were demanding, and they delivered.

We appreciate Roi-Ann Bettez's help in shaping the initial manuscript. Her questions, suggestions and editing brought order and clarity to our early meanderings.

To those who have contributed creatively over the past several months, including Justin Foster from Foster Thinking and the dozens of leaders who shaped our thinking, taught us lessons and commented on drafts throughout our writing, we say, "thank you." We are particularly grateful to Dr. Dave and Vera Mefford, who brought us together and gave us invaluable insights into applied axiology through their writing, mentoring and friendship.

We are indebted to Bill Bonnstetter and Dave Bonnstetter from TTI Success Insights, as well as their team, for the industry-leading tools they have provided us in our work with leaders for over twenty years.

The TriMetrix HD System® has been transformative, both for our clients and ourselves. They have also introduced us to more wonderful people in the fields of executive coaching, leadership development and consulting than we can capture on this page. To all of you, thanks!

The members of the Price Associates team have been encouraging and supportive throughout. They are all visible on www.price-associates. com. We owe a special thanks to Sharon Brooks, who does everything humanly possible to keep us on track and then reboots cheerfully when we get derailed anyway. She has been loyal beyond what we deserve and continues to manage our digital and public relations opportunities. Dale Dixon, CEO of the Snake River Better Business Bureau, has been a great friend and advisor for many years and was an early supporter of this work. Whit Mitchell, of Working InSync International, inspired us with his enthusiasm for this project and his conclusion that this project is just what leaders need, "beyond an MBA."

Without Ryan Lisk, Randy's son, this book probably would not have been completed. His successful transition in taking over and growing Lisk Associates would make any dad proud. Karen, Randy's wife, has been a constant burst of sunshine and encouragement to both of us. How can we do anything but succeed with her influence? And Ron continues to learn his greatest lessons about authentic leadership from his wife, Pam, six adult children and growing number of grandchildren.

Most of all, we are grateful to and for each other. We have different perspectives, styles and experiences—yet we enjoy being together. We come from very different life journeys, yet share many of the same values. We are on vastly different schedules these days, yet relish whenever they intersect. When we are together, we are clearer thinkers, we manage ourselves a bit better, and we make deeper human connections. Along with the many people who have been a vital part of this project, the past four years have served to increase our respect and love for each other.

REFERENCES

"A Message To Garcia." *Foundations Magazine*. http://www.
foundationsmag.com/garcia.html (accessed October 7,
2013).

"Anthony Robles Bio." Sun Devil Athletics.
www.thesundevils.com/ViewArticle.dbml?DB_OEM_
ID=30300&ATCLID=207923605 (accessed September 1,
2013).

Bonnstetter, Bill J. and Ashley Bowers. *Talent Unknown 7 Ways
to Discover Hidden Talent + Skills*. Scottsdale, AZ: Target
Training International, Ltd, 15th printing, 2013

Bonnstetter, Bill J. and Judy I. Suiter. *The Universal Language
DISC Reference Manual*. Scottsdale, AZ: Target Training
International, Ltd, 15th printing, 2013.

"Christopher Reeve: Biography." Christopher & Dana Reeve
Foundation. http://www.christopherreeve.org/site/c.
ddJFKRNoFiG/b.4431483/ (accessed October 7, 2013).

"Col. Rowan Tells 'How I Got the Message to General Garcia.'"
West Virginia Division of Culture and History. http://www.
wvculture.org/history/military/rowanandrew01.html
(accessed October 7, 2013).

Darling, Marilyn J. and Charles S. Parry. Executive Summary
of "From Postmortem to Living Practice: An In-Depth
Study of the Evolution of the After Action Review." Signet
Consulting. www.signetconsulting.com/downloads/aar_
execsummary.pdf (accessed September 1, 2013).

Drucker, Peter F. *The Effective Executive*. New York: Harper & Row, 1967.

Dunar, Andrew J. and Stephen P. Warring. "The *Challenger* Accident." Chap. 9 in *Power to Explore: A History of Marshall Space Flight Center 1960-1990*. Washington, DC: NASA History Office, 1999. http://history.msfc.nasa.gov/book/chptnine.pdf (accessed September 7, 2013).

"Edison's Foreign Patents." Rutgers: The Thomas Edison Papers. http://edison.rutgers.edu/dmforpat.htm (accessed October 7, 2013).

"Edison's Lightbulb." The Franklin Institute. www.fi.edu/learn/sci-tech/edison-lightbulb/edison-lightbulb.php?cts=electricity (accessed September 1, 2013).

"Education for Life and Work: Developing Transferable Knowledge and Skills in the 21st Century." The National Academies Press. http://www.nap.edu/catalog.php?record_id=13398 (accessed September 1, 2013).

"A Message to Garcia: Work, Ethics, Loyalty and Obedience." Companion material to *Elbert Hubbard: An American Original*. PBS. http://www.pbs.org/wned/elbert-hubbard/edu-work-ethics.php (accessed October 7, 2013).

Hubbard, Elbert. "A Message to Garcia." Birdsnest. http://www.birdsnest.com/garcia.htm (accessed October 7, 2013).

Hunter, John. Speech. Michigan State University, East Lansing, MI, n.d.

Isaacson, Walter. "Steve Jobs: Walter Isaacson." Amazon.com. http://www.amazon.com/Steve-Jobs-Walter-Isaacson/dp/1451648537 (accessed September 1, 2013).

Justice, Izzy. *Recovering the Spirit of Management: A Reader-Interactive Experience of Self Discovery.* Bloomington, IN: iUniverse, 2001.

Kahneman, Daniel. *Thinking, Fast and Slow.* London: Allen Lane, 2011.

Lincoln, Abraham. "Gettysburg Address." Transcription of the Lincoln Memorial text. Library of Congress. http://myloc. gov/Exhibitions/gettysburgaddress/exhibitionitems/Pages/ MemorialTranscription.html (accessed September 1, 2013).

MacIver, Rod. "Creative Work as a Way to Connect With Our Center." December eNews. Rowe Camp & Conference Center. rowecenter.org/upload/docs/RodMacIver.pdf (accessed September 26, 2013).

Mitchell, George. "Q&A with George Mitchell." By Rita Braver. CBS News. http://www.cbsnews.com/8301-3445_162-57363004/q-a-with-george-mitchell/ (accessed October 1, 2013).

Morton, Brian. "Falser Words Were Never Spoken." *New York Times*, 29 August 2011. http://www.nytimes. com/2011/08/30/opinion/falser-words-were-never-spoken. html?_r=0 (accessed September 22, 2013).

Nguyen, Courtney. "Sergiy Stakhovsky Shocks Roger Federer in Second Round of Wimbledon." Beyond the Baseline. 26 June 2013. http://tennis.si.com/2013/06/26/roger-federer-sergiy-stakhovsky-wimbledon-second-round/ (accessed October 7, 2013).

"Past Results of The Ryder Cup." PGA.com. http://www. rydercup.com/usa/history/past-results-of-the-ryder-cup (accessed September 19, 2013).

Prochnau, William W., and Laura Parker. *Miracle on the Hudson: The Extraordinary Real-life Story behind Flight 1549, by the Survivors.* New York: Ballantine Books, 2009.

Schilling, David Russell. "Knowledge Doubling Every 12 Months, Soon to be Every 12 Hours." Industry Tap. 19 April 2013. www.industrytap.com/knowledge-doubling-every-12-months-soon-to-be-every-12-hours/3950 (accessed September 1, 2013).

"Self-Knowledge, Values, And Valuations." Robert S. Hartman Institute. www.hartmaninstitute.org/self-knowledge-values-valuations/ (accessed September 26, 2013).

Senge, Peter M. *The Fifth Discipline: The Art & Practice of the Learning Organization.* New York: Doubleday/Currency, 1990.

Stenger, Richard. "Man on the Moon: Kennedy Speech Ignited the Dream." CNN.com, 28 May 2001. http://archives.cnn.com/ (accessed September 16, 2013).
"The History of the Ryder Cup." PGA.com. http://www.rydercup.com/2010/usa/history/ (accessed September 19, 2013).

"The Xerox Problem Solving Process." Farmer Business Systems. http://www.farmerbusiness.com/blog/the-xerox-problem-solving-process/ (accessed October 7, 2013).

INDEX

GROWING INFLUENCE: A STORY OF HOW TO LEAD WITH CHARACTER, EXPERTISE, AND IMPACT

by Ron Price and Stacy Ennis

Leadership is about influence.

Emily is a career-driven thirtysome-thing who is making an impact as a leader at a tech company, but after being passed up for multiple promo-tions, she finds herself at a loss for how to improve. Fate answers her in the form of a kind—and surprisingly direct—older man whom she meets in a coffee shop.

Growing Influence offers practical advice on how to develop leader-ship skills and a relatable account of one woman's growth.

THE INNOVATOR'S ADVANTAGE: REVEALING THE HIDDEN CONNECTION BETWEEN PEOPLE AND PROCESS

by Evans Baiya, PhD and Ron Price

Innovation is not just about technical and systematic processes.

In *The Innovator's Advantage*, authors Evans Baiya and Ron Price reveal that the key to success is understanding how each person's talent, skills, and passion will influence innovation. Placing the right people and maximizing their contributions is the secret to improving your innovation track record, creating in-de-mand products and services, and developing organizations where people want to work.

Learn more at TheInnovatorsAdvantage.com.

OPTIMIZING STRATEGY FOR RESULTS: A STRUCTURED APPROACH TO MAKE YOUR BUSINESS COME ALIVE

by Timothy Mwololo Waema, Ph.D., Ron Price, and Evans Baiya, Ph.D.

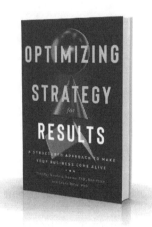

From foundation to fully optimized

When it comes to creating and implementing a strategy for an organization, the "how" and "what" of strategic planning can be elusive. In their book, *Optimizing Strategy for Results*, authors Waema, Price, and Baiya give leaders the tools, processes, and step-by-step instructions to establish a framework, create a culture, and leverage the talent, skills, and passions of their people to execute a strategy.

Learn more at OptimizingStrategyforResults.com.

REALTIME COACHING: A SIMPLE, PRACTICAL APPROACH FOR PEOPLE WHO RELY ON OTHERS TO CREATE RESULTS

by Randy Lisk and Ryan Lisk

Achieve your goals by helping others achieve theirs.

RealTime Coaching is a simple, practical approach to working with others. The approach you will learn is friendly, firm, and fair—and it works. A RealTime coach works with the assumption that both the needs of the person and the organization are important. This win-win approach taps the true source of individual power: intrinsic motivation.

TREASURE INSIDE: 23 UNEXPECTED PRINCIPLES THAT ACTIVATE GREATNESS

by Ron Price

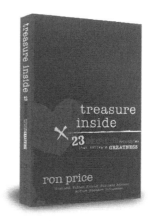

**Greatness lies within you.
It is there . . . waiting for you to discover it.**

Internationally recognized author, speaker, and business advisor Ron Price has discovered the secret to human potential. Inspirational, practical, and thought provoking, *Treasure Inside's* true value is in helping you recognize that these great treasures reside inside you. Discover these 23 principles—from the sanctity of silence to the power of faith—and let *Treasure Inside* be a catalyst for leading a life extraordinary.

BUMPER STICKER LEADERSHIP: ONE-LINER WISDOM ON LIFE AND BUSINI

by Randy Lisk

Life is a learning experience only if you learn.
—Yogi Berra

Bumper stickers were social media before Twitter ever tweeted. Executive coach, consultant, and author Randy Lisk distills his over 40 years of experience in business into bumper stickers for your personal and team development. Randy breaks down the complexities of leadership into simple, practical and profound statements.

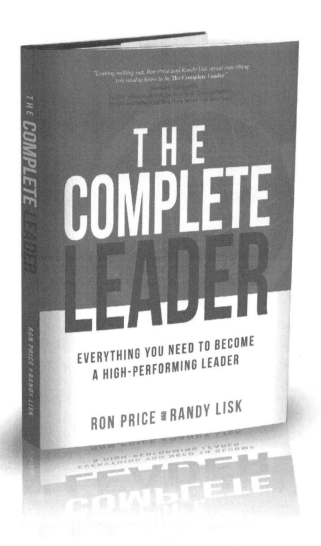

**JOIN THE COMPLETE LEADER COMMUNITY AT THECOMPLETELEADER.ORG
TO CONTINUE YOUR JOURNEY TO BECOMING A HIGH-PERFORMING LEADER.**

With the purchase of this book, you will receive a complimentary six-month membership to The Complete Leader Community, with access to additional resources, tools and a leadership assessment. Simply email info@TheCompleteLeader.org with proof of purchase, and you will receive your access code.

ABOUT THE AUTHORS

Ron Price currently serves as the president of TTI Success Insights, a company that is dedicated to revealing human potential in workplaces across the globe. In 2004, Ron founded Price Associates, a global leadership performance firm. Drawing from his travels and over thirty-five years of experience in leading successful organizations, Ron brings a unique perspective to developing talent and bringing out the best in ourselves and others. Ron and his wife, Pam, live in Boise, Idaho, and have six children and ten grandchildren.

Randy Lisk is the founder of Lisk Associates, consultants to business. Today, Lisk Associates is owned and operated by his son, Ryan Lisk. Randy has a bachelor's and master's degree in electrical engineering, which he utilized in his twenty-three-year career at IBM. He has had a broad impact in multiple industries as a trusted advisor, consultant and coach since leaving his corporate position with IBM in 1991. Randy has designed and presented supervisor and leadership education; taught coaching, communications and leadership skills to managers; helped teams reach their goals; and positively impacted the lives of thousands of people. During a workshop in Europe, an Italian manager called Randy, "A positive virus which should be spread." Randy and his wife, Karen, are now retired and enjoy spending their time collecting shells and taking photos on Sanibel Island, Florida.

Made in the USA
Middletown, DE
17 October 2023

40977257R00191